*Zapping*

*through*

*Wonderland*

# *Zapping*

# *through*

# *Wonderland*

*Social issues in art for children and young people*

Edited by Colin Prescod

ROYAL TROPICAL INSTITUTE - THE NETHERLANDS

*Zapping through Wonderland: social issues in art for children and young people* is a co-production of the Royal Tropical Institute, the Foundation Arts and Young People in Europe and the European Cultural Foundation, all located in Amsterdam. Financial and moral support has been provided by the Dutch Ministry of Cultural Affairs, the Dutch Ministry of Foreign Affairs and the European Cultural Foundation.

Royal Tropical Institute
PO Box 95001
1090 HA Amsterdam
The Netherlands
Tel: (31) 20 - 56 88 272
Fax: (31) 20 - 56 88 286
Email: kitpress@kit.nl

ISBN 90 6832 287 7
NUGI 661/911

P

Why did children and young people across Europe massively attend the play *Mirad, a Boy from Bosnia*, a play on the effects of war on families and children and on the plight of refugees across Europe? Can art help children and young people address important social issues? And if so, how can adult artists make productions that make a difference to young people and combine social commitment with high artistic criteria?

Inspired by the success of the play *Mirad, a Boy from Bosnia* by Ad de Bont, EU NET ART (the Foundation Arts and Young People in Europe) and the European Cultural Foundation organized, in May 1997, the project *Ouch! Theatre Meets Social Reality.* Leading theatre-makers and young playwrights sought to bridge the gap between aesthetics and social commitment and to explore the interaction between youth, art and social developments in Europe. The enthusiasm of the participants led the organizers to raise this question again among artists from various disciplines, including film, visual arts, theatre and museums. The expert meeting *Through the Looking Glass: Arts, Youth and Culture in Europe,* which took place in Amsterdam in April 1998, and this book are the tangible results of our efforts.

EU NET ART and the European Cultural Foundation believe that the arts can offer challenging opportunities to young people to learn and express themselves, to expand their social and personal development and to communicate with others. Self-expression and communication are increasingly important in societies which are subject to social and cultural change.

The partnership between EU NET ART and the European Cultural Foundation is a natural outgrowth of our common concern for cultural cooperation in Europe. It manifests the importance of cross-border and cross-cultural networking, of interdisciplinary exchange and open, non-hierarchical cooperation.

EU NET ART is a European network of some 90 professional arts organizations covering all art disciplines and with members in 24 countries across Western, Central and Eastern Europe. The overall aim of EU NET ART is to create more space for arts activities for children and young people in Europe and to develop an arts environment sympathetic to the needs of children and young people. The activities of EU NET ART facilitate the exchange of ideas and experiences between professional artists working for these specific audiences and encourage children and young people to explore their own creativity.

The European Cultural Foundation, which was established in 1954 to stimulate a cultural dimension in the post-war movement towards European integration, aims to promote cultural cooperation in Europe. The European Cultural Foundation interlinks its grants and programme policies enabling it to develop and maintain in-house and partnership programmes as well as to support external projects. It does so within set priority areas which reflect topical developments in Europe. The priority areas are currently: Central and Eastern Europe; the Mediterranean region; and cultural pluralism. This particular publication was developed within the framework of the ECF project *Art for Social Change* (priority: cultural pluralism), a project for artists who help young people empower themselves through the artistic process with a special focus on the child's social context.

We are very fortunate to have found in Colin Prescod the spirit and wisdom needed to moderate the expert meeting *Through the Looking Glass* and to edit the contributions to *Zapping through Wonderland*. Born in Trinidad in 1944, Colin Prescod became resident in the United Kingdom in 1958. His active involvement in youth and race issues, his academic background in sociology and his creative work in film and television combine into a powerful mix of creativity, expertise and commitment.

The artists and art providers who participated in this creative enterprise were invited based on the daring exploration of social issues in their work for children and young people. Obviously many other, equally interesting art projects could have been gathered. We hope there will be an opportunity to do so in the future. A conscious effort has been made to include various art disciplines and to cover different regions in Europe. The essayists were invited to contribute views "from the outside looking in" on this field of artistic activity, from radically different approaches and disciplines, thereby broadening the scope of the discussion.

The organizers would like to thank the Dutch Ministries of Culture and of Foreign Affairs for their generous contribution through the HGIS funds for international cultural relations. Without their financial and moral support this project could not have been realized. We hope other governmental organizations as well as private and corporate foundations will realize the importance of actively stimulating the arts for children and young people, and sow the seeds of cultural and social awareness in the European citizens of tomorrow.

At the same time our heartful thanks go to the artists and project managers who have participated in our meetings and whose art work for children and young people you will find presented in this book. It is their conviction that art can make a difference in the lives of children and young people and their decision to devote their artistic careers to this purpose that have inspired us to make this publication.

May this book stimulate readers to further explore this particular artistic field. The expert meeting and this publication are prime examples of the platform function of networks such as EU NET ART. Networks are informal and open meeting places for the exchange of experiences, artistic growth and professional development: feel welcome to join.

On behalf of EU NET ART and the European Cultural Foundation,

*Anne van Otterloo, Erica Kubic and Veronie Willemars*

Editor's

The reader of this publication will find reference to madness, drugs, sex, deadly diseases, physical brutality, war, alienation and anarchy. All this in a book that addresses social issues in art for children and young people, from the perspective of artists and art providers. At the centre of its concern is "childhood". However, the concern is not with childhood as a taken for granted, natural, biological fact or social institution. Rather, it is with childhood as a socially defined, always shifting "space" - in fact, childhood as a contested terrain.

One of the twentieth century's main claims to distinctiveness is that it has been marked by extraordinarily rapid change. The industrial revolution, firmly established by the late nineteenth century, laid the foundation for an accelerated pace of social change. Epitomized by the technological which has expanded material possibilities, this revolution was, however, directed and driven by the dominant social forces and contradictions that have characterized the increasing industrial capitalist domination of the globe. The twentieth century has been marked by a quiet hysteria about the rapidity of this change, particularly where these changes have thrown up unforeseen and disturbing contradictions. So the twentieth century has been as much about the courage of mass societies to face up to the problematic, uncomfortable and sometimes devastating consequences of changes that we ourselves have set in motion.

We live then with the constant menacing feeling that change has got out of hand. But although there are late twentieth century schools of thought or philosophies that speak of our era as the end of history, in the main we have not given up the belief that we can still do something about this situation - contentious and problematic though many of the issues are.

Even so, and partly because of the sheer magnitude of some of these contradictions and challenges, it is noticeable that our societies are characterized by partial and arbitrary application to them. It is, in fact, largely the politicians and officials of the state who dominate the setting of the agenda on facing up to the contradictions. But it is also evident that this agenda can be influenced by forces from other sectors of society. In this publication we look at the practice of artists and art providers who are engaged in what might be called art strategies for influencing our ability to apprehend and possibly to do something about our discomfiting social predicaments often euphemistically referred to as "social issues".

In spring 1998, the European Cultural Foundation enlisted the support of the Foundation Arts and Young People in Europe (EU NET ART) to set up what was rather intimidatingly called an "expert-meeting", in Amsterdam, under the title *Through the Looking Glass: Art, Youth and Culture in Europe*. It was to be a cross-arts and cross-philosophies assembly. It was very self-consciously a creative, risk-taking enterprise - a "be-in" for the participants, all with noteworthy, outstanding achievements in their different artistic and professional fields. I was invited to moderate the two-day assembly and to take the lead responsibility in editing a text which was one of the anticipated outcomes of this meeting. So the main wished-for and wishful outcomes of this exciting assembly were firstly, to stir new work and better-informed approaches amongst the immediate participants and secondly, to generate a publication that might spread the word. Not surprisingly, this publication marks then not a completion but a starting point, with provocatively open questions, tantalizing suggestions and fruitful admissions of ignorance.

Attending the "expert-meeting" were representatives of work from museums, theatre and the visual arts including film and video (with the regrettable absence of the new art practices in the virtual reality worlds of the digital electronic media). They had come from all corners of Europe to celebrate their successes, to admit to the challenges with which they still battle, to air uncertainties and to reflect on the necessity of risk and the fascination with unanticipated even if sometimes discomfiting outcomes. In spite of all the differences between them, what very quickly became established was that they were united as artists, dreaming and imagining in a rapidly changing world full of social contradiction, for children and the young. Each of them has their personal reason and route for becoming involved with work for children and the young. But for all of them there must be a kind of calling to touch and connect with something of the spirit of the next world, the new world, tomorrow's world - the world as it will be defined by the next generation. And for all of them, as though by instinct, they find themselves exercising a responsibility to pass on what they know or what they intuit about delighting in the senses - brushing up the synapses, in order to engage, through the feelings, with strange and disturbing matters in the wild garden of childhood experience.

In truth, this publication is arguably a rather restrictive form of conveying, in particular, the excitement and achievements of the artists and their works, since the reader cannot see and be touched by the physical art works around which discussion revolves. In a sense then, the text is a space for notes and thoughts to be followed up. Assembled here are reports and reflections on 11, socially engaged art works and projects from those associated with making or exhibiting them. And to accompany these reports, four essayists, invited to provoke and surprise, present bold and experimental utterances about the social trends and controversies that sketch in some parts of the context and against which art interventions impact.

The works discussed in the reports section of the book deal with a number of challenging contemporary social issues - among them bullying, drug abuse, AIDS, rape, psychosis, and living with difference in the new Europe, at the crossroads of global migrations. Each report is headed by the title of the art project and name of the "expert" person, artist or art provider, responsible for the work discussed. And each one is comprised of an introduction and presentation, extracted from statements by the artist or art provider, and a reflection, constructed so as to underline contentious and unresolved matters related to the work and raised by the person representing the project at the meeting or by other participants in discussion on the work. The essays function as an oblique complement to the reports. They represent dis-orienting and re-orienting ways of thinking about the big factors in play that test and constrain the skill and imagination of all those who take up the responsibility of communicating to or with children and the young.

Thomas Ziehe and Maura Dooley, in very different styles, are both eloquent about the changing form and content of what constitutes childhood in our times. Here the excesses of popular culture, fuelled as much by commerce and industry as by the crises in the political and social institutions of mass society, present us with new generations of young people whose behaviours and expectations confound the standards of older generations. There is a disturbing question raised implicitly by both Ziehe and Dooley. How are adults to exercise a responsibility to and for children who live almost literally in another world from them? The creativity and imagination of artists could just prove vital in mediating, to use an image from Maura Dooley, between the haven of mum and the dangers of the wild garden. Thomas Ziehe's sociological essay, focuses on the "informalization", "ambivalence" and information invasion which characterize today's youth culture and which therefore menace childhood. It is followed by reports on the startlingly experimental Belgian theatre-making company, Victoria; the HIV/AIDS visual arts exhibition, curated at the Walsall Museum in the United Kingdom; and Suzanne Osten's triumphant drama about parental madness, *The Girl, the Mother and the Trash*, as performed by her Unga Klara company in Stockholm. While Maura Dooley's boldly impressionistic piece about the in-scape of childhood, points us to the reports on the very special theatrical intervention of the Oxford Stage Company, under the directorship of John Retallack - the grand project of which is to manage a transfusion of some fresh dramatic blood into the corpus of English theatre for children; the long-standing and still insurgent, roaming theatre of O Bando in Portugal, represented here by founder-member Raul Atalaia; and the award-winning film work of Maria Peters, from the Netherlands.

The essays by Mohammed Benzakour and Pál Békés are commentaries, again in very different styles, on the shifting and shifted broad cultural context within which artists and art providers find themselves attempting to reach and influence the young. The new Europe is characterized by movement, between cultures, across borders, from one era to another with great rapidity - in global migrations, in the shift from the old to the new world order, in the demise of established hegemonies faced with new pop-hegemonic challenges and claims. These are the features of what I have called elsewhere an "all-change world". These are the changes and shifts that constitute a truly dynamic multiculturalism in contemporary Europe. Mohammed Benzakour's strident declamations, spinning off the theme of multiculture, combine and collide with the reports on Marlene Schneider's multi-media work on the experience of migrants; the much-visited museum installation on Bolivian myth and culture, mounted by the Children's Museum at the Royal Tropical Institute in Amsterdam; and the experimental visual arts work of RASA, in Belgium, under the pioneering directorship of Gerd Dierckx. And Pál Békés' letter from a rapidly changing Hungary, turning on his experience as a television producer of modern tales for children, accompanies the reports from engaged Finnish film maker Raimo O Niemi; and the barrier-breaking Berlin Film Festival for Children, under its director Renate Zylla.

Quite apart from the work discussed, the participants explore issues around the actual process of doing their work - in relations with funding, funders and the market; the working and re-working of old stories in a world turned post-modern; the spread of fast-edit, clip-culture which seems to militate against slow linear narratives; activating children as participant art-work makers. Amongst all the challenges to the effectiveness of their practice, perhaps the major threat to the proficiency of adults involved with art for children and the young and dealing with social issues is posed by the tendency to fall into what might be called the pedagogical imperative. There has always been a suspicion that the pursuit of "true", "quality" or "great" art is compromised by any didactic inclination to deliver messages or meanings. In one way or another, all the artists represented in this publication have taken up the challenge of avoiding mere pedagogy in their social issues work, and won. The trick, we learn, is to make work that poses new and fresh questions for children to explore - holding short of imposing answers, our answers.

**Thomas Ziehe**

# EVERYDAY CULTURE AND THE FORMATION OF IDENTITY

*Young people and the process of cultural modernization*

### A new outlook on life: everyday culture

Our experience of everyday life has been transformed. And since we are so closely involved in the process of transformation, little by little, day by day, we tend to lose sight of the momentous scale of the changes that are taking place. This is especially true when we look at the lives of children and young people today. The culture they grow up in, the culture they encounter on a daily basis has been pervasively modernized. Indeed, from their point of view, the only type of culture which young people have been able to experience in their lifetimes is thoroughly modernistic.

This everyday culture, imbued with the values of modernism, is a loosely woven tapestry of issues, images, senses of direction, ways of perception, fads and fashions, a re-evaluation of what external objects mean. It has itself become an agent for cultural change: it enables children and young people to relate themselves to the lives they lead. Teenage magazines are able to impart to its readership a whole range of behavioural and evaluative standards which go a long way towards shaping the value systems of the young individual. This is quite evident in the extensive coverage of readers' letters.

The modernized everyday culture is all-pervasive, it seeps into the pores of peoples' lifestyles and mentalities and therefore cannot be narrowed down to a single "field of activity" such as leisure. It has an impact on all layers of society, on the middle classes in which it competes with the handing down of traditional high culture, on the lower classes in which it eclipses working class and neighbourhood traditions and in migrant communities in which young people value popular culture as a counterweight against the expectations and traditions of their parents.

There is an ever-widening gap between a mentality which has evolved within children and young people as a result of the everyday culture on the one hand and the educational intentions of teachers on the other. It is becoming increasingly difficult for both sides to summon up the motivation to bridge this gap. Although the job of the teacher is now to bridge this gap, when trying to do so she or he can no longer rely on what once went without saying: namely that both sides were united in sharing the norms and values of high-brow culture.

### Secondary modernization
Another noteworthy aspect of everyday culture is that we have become accustomed to the way in which it has dismantled the old traditions. We no longer feel that there is anything radically new about this, in fact we have stopped finding this intrinsically strange or even exciting. This peculiar sensation - that everyday culture is no longer celebrated as a break with the "traditional" times of old, that modernity no longer induces feelings of astonishment, of giddiness, of feverish excitement - would seem to support the plausibility of the notion that our current stage of social development is best described as a second modernization (and in

the same way, other authors speak of late modernism, post-modernism or reflexive modernization).

Put simply, the first phase of modernization consists of social improvements in efficiency and cultural processes of rationalization. In the second phase of modernization these developments have already been completely assimilated, they have lost their magic and become trivialized. The resultant effect which all this has on our view on life is considerable: to take just one example, if we go back to the first phase of modernization we can remember how an all-glass, new school building was seen as a necessary condition for the cultivation of happy, bright and healthy minds and bodies in young students. You could almost say that that was the "Kennedy effect" of an attitude which embraced modernization and all it stood for, say, in 1961. But if we move on to the second phase of modernization, i.e. today, and revisit the same school building, then it is not just the plaster which is literally coming unstuck; no, the way we feel and think has changed, too. These days nobody would seriously expect a new building to be able almost to automatically invoke a permanent sense of joy among those who use it.

*Everyday culture is no longer celebrated as a break with the "traditional" times of old*

The point that I'm trying to make is this: young people's view on life in the second phase of modernization is different. They are much less likely to get carried away by anything which calls itself "new", their view on life is more fragmented, more pragmatic, more disillusioned than before. Modernization, or more precisely the artefacts of modernization, no longer give rise to euphoric expectations among the young, the majority of whom no longer perceive modernization as an enrichment of their lives.

All of this, of course, has considerable consequences for people's day to day work in educational institutions, for example in schools. During the first phase of modernization the issues were clear: the struggle to break with tradition, the confrontation with the representatives of authority, with the adult world, firstly in the form of "pranks" - something which almost has a nostalgic ring to it today - then later in the form of emotionally highly-charged political "events" and "campaigns". Amongst young people a common view on life and time spent in school was that it meant nothing more than to continually suffer from the fact that "everything is forbidden, so you can't do that". The central conflict was one of repression. For the more fortunate ones, getting older meant getting rid of the straitjacket which the forces of tradition had come to symbolize.

In the second phase of modernization the terms of reference have shifted considerably. Neither parents nor teachers of the young today can rely on a "traditional" upbringing. The pivotal conflict for teenagers of today does not reside in the question of how to deal with the suffering engendered by a series of prohibitions, but in trying to come to terms with what a young person is supposed to make of his or her life. Consequently, the issue of repression has given way to the questions: "What am I here for?" and even "What is the point of my being here?", i.e. issues of existential and motivational significance. In today's world it becomes increasingly difficult for a young person to define his or her identity in terms of what he or she is "against". Instead, the question that he or she is attempting to answer is more like: "Well, what is it that I would like to be, that I am in favour of?"

The difficulty arises when we come to consider the educationalists who, now approaching middle-age, were shaped by the first phase of modernization and would still like to believe that today's youth shares their former dreams and aspirations. After all, shouldn't young people be grateful that the old traditions have disappeared, that even school has become a much more liberal place to be in? But what do the kids of the second phase of modernization go and do? They ask the teacher: Please Miss, why do *we* have to choose what we're going to do today?

## *A share in modernization: changing notions of youth*

Everyday culture and the second phase of modernization have all acted to produce an environment within which the way young people relate to the way they live their lives has changed. On the one hand, young people can remain "young" for longer than ever before, even though on the other they are no longer "young" in the classical sense of the word. This means that the aspirations of the adolescent have, in a peculiar sense, become appropriated by society at large. They have become stereotypical components of everyday culture. For this reason, and as paradoxical as it might seem, we can maintain two things at the same time: today's everyday culture would seem to contain a "youthful" dimension, even though the young people of today appear to become part of the adult everyday culture at an ever earlier age. I would like to indicate just how this early inclusion into the world of adults can be both edifying and disparaging for young people.

## *Setting the agenda: unlimited access to information*

I can begin by saying that it has become a cultural commonplace that we are today able to access information on all of the burning issues in society. Whether the talk is of serious catastrophes, global risks or even new products, fads and fashions or new trends, the fact is that everyone can inform themselves about almost any topic under the sun. Even those secretive aspects of early puberty, sexuality and the psyche now present themselves as issues which can be discussed openly and without fear of reprimand. Today's young people no longer have to put up a fight to gain access to the issues that concern them. Each and every private TV channel is able to provide a constant background of images and visual shreds, the voyeuristic quality of which reproduces the old pubescent keyhole perspective by the means of mass communication. Of course this signifies a partial victory for young people: parents and teachers have largely given up on their role of shielding the young from "adult" issues; the goalposts have been left wide open.

But there is a price to be paid for all of this; having to somehow shield oneself from the excessive quantity of information which is being transmitted. It is as if the piles of visual data, information and issues have to be kept at arms length by the young people of today in order that their attempts to assert their own identity are not buried or stifled at birth, in order that they can experience and maintain the personal significance of their own small life history.

*To bicker over one's own sense of identity, to constantly ask oneself what the meaning of life can possibly be*

## Informalization

Turning towards the next phenomenon: our culture has tacitly looked on whilst traditional social forms have slowly disintegrated and run down. But it is not so much young people who act to undermine and remove traditions with each passing day; rather it is the middle-aged generation - in other words their parents. In general, the new generation of parents does its best to remove the disciplinary element from bringing up children: the palette extends from no more sitting up straight to having to have neat handwriting, from wearing Sunday clothes to having to attend at formal visits, from Catechism to the private house party. In each and every case informalization proved to be victorious. One's own parents go on holiday wearing tracksuits, while even the Customs and Immigration people have had their ears pierced.

The downside of informalization is that it goes hand in hand with considerable perceptual confusion. That means that in comparison with earlier times there are many more situations upon which more than one process appears to operate, situations which appear transparent to the outside observer and yet which can be interrupted at any time or which can "bomb" at any moment. I am referring to a phenomenon which teachers know only too well from their gut instincts: in reality, nothing is impossible within the confines of the classroom, in reality "anything" can happen.

What used to be taken as informality amongst young people has now been subsumed into an altogether wider everyday culture. It is no longer necessary to fight for the right to be informal; informalization itself forms a self-evident part of the cultural context. For this reason it is quite possible that certain young people could express the - at first sight contradictory - wish to hold a school-leaving party "formal dress required". By doing so, the jeans-clad teacher is left in a quandary of whether to don a shirt and tie or go for that "formal" skirt. It would appear that this is another feather in the cap for the modernists, since it looks as if young people can choose the degree of formality they believe is appropriate to the occasion. After all, formal attire is just one form of dress amongst many. There is, however, also another side to this coin. What used to be dictated by formal social norms and behaviour is now dependent on the motivational whim of the individual. In place of conventional pressure, it is the individual who needs to perform and this gives rise to a general sense of unease, delay and circumvention. The fact remains that informalization remains an integral feature of the everyday culture but in return requires an equal and opposite counterweight of the individual's own ability to become motivated.

### Exploring the inner world

I will touch on a final point: within our culture it has now become completely acceptable to follow and indeed flounder about in one's own private world. To bicker over one's own sense of identity, to constantly ask oneself what the meaning of life can possibly be, and all of this in the form of a persistent dialogue with one's inner self: no longer can this be viewed as the tortuous and secretive domain of pubescent diarists. No, this form of self-disclosure is just part of the tools that go to make up the personalities of architects, buyers, workshop participants, clients of mainstream Adult Education Institutes and teachers. The walls surrounding the diarist's self-centred reflections have begun to crumble and fall away, such egocentricity is no longer the preserve of the pubescent adolescent nor the object of literary research. Instead, adopting a purely subjective point of view has become a fact of life when it comes to our perceptions of ourselves and the world around us. Put somewhat sarcastically we might say that someone sets fire to the local theatre "in order to be noticed". But we would hardly be exaggerating in saying that we now expect everyone else to be able to talk about their own feelings, fears and desires – and if they can't, then God knows, but only a course of therapy will be able to save them.

*Frequently nowadays the path towards self-discovery can no longer be placed within the context of an adventure trail*

The point is that subjectivization is no longer a demand which must be reclaimed and fought for by euphoric young people with a frisson of excitement from an indifferent adult world. It has become an expression of the individual's lifestyle, to be approved or disapproved of at will, but it certainly is no longer something which today's young people must strive to discover or attain. However, the fact that young people are able to set out on their journey through life with such a high – and positively reinforced – degree of subjectivism is something which I believe is a victory for the side of modernity.

Conversely, I believe that the downside of all this lies in the fact that such subjectivity is no longer able to evoke feelings of euphoria because it no longer possesses the aura of what is new. "She has managed to find her inner self", someone says of a young woman. "Well, I hope she's not too disappointed", says the other. Frequently nowadays the path towards self-discovery can no longer be placed within the context of an adventure trail but within the pages of a semantic package-holiday. The longing to explore one's inner world has, in the case of many young people, become replaced by the longing to be able to handle the emotionally downward spiral perceived in one's own internal film. But for a significantly large section of young people the cultural opportunity for self-observation has led to a desperate dependency on others to provide confirmation of one's own self-regard: "I've gotta get back to myself" - as the somewhat convoluted jargon goes - is in reality only possible for many if they seek and find the approval of others.

### Self-empowerment or trivialization

I hope that these three aspects of setting the agenda, informalization and subjectivization have made it quite clear: youth phenomena have long become an integral part of what I call everyday culture, and, at the same time, everyday culture has had a significant effect on young people.

It would appear that today's young people are freely able to maintain their emotions and perceptions gained during puberty for a much longer period than before, although in reality this only holds true if such emotions and perceptions can be reflected in the adult world. However the complexity and the multiplicity of ways which the individual has at their disposal in order to deal with this subject matter is such that at this stage I can draw no definitive conclusions. Nonetheless it should be stated that the issue is deeply ambiguous, since the same data may be used to support the arguments of either self-empowerment or self-trivialization of young people.

I use the term self-empowerment in the sense that young people are able to set the cultural agenda, they are innately aware of the processes of informalization and subjectivization and that the door to the adult world has been left more transparent, more open than ever before in the last two centuries of modernism. There are many who can derive some sense of recognition, awareness and strength from all of this. But at the same time the everyday culture can lead to a trivialization of oneself, especially since the cultural reflection of personal destinies sometimes falls short of the mark. It certainly isn't easy to experience oneself in such a naked context as original, new and open to the future.

The perceptual perspective of young people is strongly marked by their own egocentricity or selfishness. There is a certain danger that such vulnerability runs the risk of becoming embedded in the dominant culture or that the same culture allows such behaviour over a long period of time. People who prefer to refer to themselves rather than the world about them tend to insinuate that the world about them is "just how I see my life". Yet the relationship between youth and culture cannot be seen in terms of alienation with the possibility of a curtain-saving all-embracing "rapprochement". In reality, the cultural retrospective - and I mean by that the ability to set the agenda, the topics of informalization, of subjectivization - appears so compelling that many young people are not only able to find confirmation of their general view of life but wish their dreams to become true, preferably sooner than later. We can slowly observe a trend, tacitly encouraged by the predominant culture, amongst children and young people to prematurely secure their identities (Erik Erikson). This premature identification has, however, little or nothing to do with the adult perspective. On the contrary, the identification refers more to a cognitive and emotional fixation on the image the young person has of him- or herself or on the somewhat blinkered view which the young person has of his or her perceptual habits.

### Aesthetic experience: a confrontation with strangeness

Our new everyday culture is full of aesthetic experiences. We need only think of how we have grown accustomed to the fact that all clothing is styled, retail outlets are designed and media messages are supported by a professional lay-out. Young people consider it to be normal that these things are part of their environment. On a concluding note, I would like to add, however, that aesthetic experiences can also function in a different way, in the sense that rather than confirming or reinforcing our habits which have sprung from everyday culture, they can offer a counter balance to these. I am not alluding to a heroic concept of high art which frowns on everyday experiences, but to an aesthetic experience which offsets the supremacy of everyday habits. I am not referring to an art that wants to be higher, but one that wants to be different.

Aesthetic processes can facilitate an introduction to a certain dose of strangeness. One could argue that it is precisely young people's apparent understanding of the world, which falsely impresses us as self-evident, that has become a problem. Aesthetics can change our outlook on life, can take away that degree of matter of course understanding of the world, can contribute to unfamiliarity and thereby to a different way of perceiving the world around us. Aesthetic experiences can also help in the social realm by offering a counterweight against trivial informalization. They make us more aware of the way we shape events in our society through rituals, stagings and styling and make us more sensitive to the social atmosphere; they can offer a counterweight against everyday habits. If young people have grown accustomed to living primarily by the priorities they have derived from everyday culture, it is important to look at how young people experience themselves. It can be a meaningful experience to leave our personal preferences behind for a while because an aesthetic work process requires it of us, because an image, a piece of music, a text is for this moment more important. It is about the ability to ask whether we really want to follow our first spontaneous impulses. It is about being able to construct and experience inner limits and the pleasure of knowing that we are not being held down by our needs and motives precisely because they can be changed. In this manner, aesthetic experiences can also allow us to temporarily take a "strange" look at our own selves. Not to find ourselves back at the same spot as before may in fact be exactly what we wanted to reach. In this way we can build small islands in the sea of everyday culture, not a pathetic counter-world, but new land.

*Build small islands in the sea of everyday culture, not a pathetic counter-world, but new land*

27

*Prof. Dr. Thomas Ziehe (Germany, 1947) has been Professor at the Institut für Pädagogik of the Universität Hannover since 1993 and Chairman of the Faculty of Education since 1997. Between 1988 and 1993 he was Professor at the Universität Frankfurt/Main.*

# Victoria

**Scene from *Kung Fu***

artist **Koen Gisen**

Koen Gisen (Belgium, 1966) is one of the core staff members of the theatre production centre Victoria and is responsible for the company's public relations.

introduction   Victoria, set up in 1992 in Ghent (Flanders), is a theatre production centre which, under the artistic leadership of Dirk Pauwels, functions as a travelling theatre company. One of the characteristics of Victoria is its choice of investing in "performing artists". The result of this is that the company has no permanent body of actors, but over the years has surrounded itself with a pool of artists. A long stream of them work or have worked in association with the company at various levels. Currently, a core staff of four decides on all policy and artistic matters.

The company works with a bold and innovative structure and process - with flexibility and risk at the core of its activities. In addition to producing medium and large-scale plays created by experienced theatre artists, and intended for touring, the company also ventures into creations by young artists and those making their first appearance.
On top of this, Victoria regularly commissions young theatre artists for smaller, one-off theatre projects, which are usually presented at the popular, annual Victoria Festival.

**Scene from *Bernadetje***

Out of this imaginative mix, Victoria has created a kind of melting pot in which often fruitful confrontations occur - between various disciplines, experienced and inexperienced makers, professional makers and non-professional actors, foreigners and citizens of Ghent, adults, adolescents and children and so on and so on. In 1997 the company managed to give more than two hundred of its own performances (30%) abroad. It makes only one big production a year in fact, so that this extraordinarily high output is one of the outcomes of the way in which its several levels of activity combine to produce added value at each level.

The company's work is aimed, for the most part, at young audiences (15 to 25 years old). Since Victoria is constantly involved in producing "young work" for young audiences, often with young people from all social layers, it is inevitable that social themes creep into its performances and all the preparatory working processes. It is, however, by no means a goal for Victoria to produce theatre performances where social matters are explicitly the main theme. Even so, since most of the company's large A-productions are set in working class environments they came to reflect social issues important in contemporary society.

The outstandingly successful play *Moeder & Kind* (Mother & Child, 1995) by Alain Platel and Arne Sierens epitomizes Victoria's style and accomplishment. The play was prompted by walks in the notorious working-class neighbourhood De Brugse Poort in Ghent (where author Arne Sierens spent his youth) and by a photo book Living Room by Nick Waplington, a colletion of photographs about family life in working-class families in the United Kingdom. It resulted in a play which confronted the audience with a slice of hyper-realistically staged, everyday-working-class-family-life in all its aspects - where five scenarios are in progress simultaneously. It turned out to be shocking and confronting, as well as very touching for some people (especially for those who had grown up in such families), because it revealed the undeniable beauty and love and creativity in the several levels of relationship found in any working class community - something transcending the taken for granted label "working-class".

Equally successful, *Bernadetje* (1997) - by the same authors - is a play that was staged on real (fair-ground) "dodgems". Once again, the characters were very "working-class", the language on stage was very "colloquial" and still it was an implicit ode to the desires, ambitions and struggles for life of the portrayed.

Scene from *Bernadetje*

Many of the anecdotes and situations in the play were extracted from the players' real lives and personal experience, elaborated through improvisations. The authors of both plays emphasize that in their work they function as seismographs (a device to measure the movements of the Earth's crust, in this case of contemporary society), hence they make chronicles of contemporary everyday life. Their comment, or better, their statement, is simply to stage this culturally marginalized social class, its values and its much disowned aesthetics. Neither of the plays has a "proper storyline".

Another example of this particular method of dealing with social matters is perhaps Victoria's latest production *WYSIWYG* (What You See Is What You Get), (1998), by young author Paul Mennes and director Peter van den Eede. In this play, Mennes discusses people's decreasing ability to communicate with each other and the role of the new media in this process. Mennes has been considered by many, mainly young, people as the leading mouthpiece of a new generation, "...one who is able to capture in exact detail the everyday life of the nineties". His main themes are communication, media, boredom, drug abuse and several other aspects of the middle-class youth culture that can touch and sometimes cross into working class youth culture. This "chroniqueurship" is precisely the reason why Victoria, in its role as a producer, wished to commission him to write a play.

reflection        There is a sense in which the theatre-making of Victoria neutralizes and makes redundant traditional theatre commentary and critique. This arises from the reflexive, self-critiqueing, self-awareness of its entire structure and process. The company's art work steps outside of the framework of the usual objectives. It is not intimidated by objections to what it intends as challenges for its audiences. It engages its audiences in the risk of failure for its fresh and exploratory work. It surrenders to the flow and contradiction of what Thomas Ziehe calls "everyday culture". It makes a theatre-making technique of the TV "zap", fast change, short concentration span phenomenon that so appals "the older generation". It surfs the tidal wave of information overkill, fearlessly.

The company's worrying concerns are about "keeping the faith": not betraying its demanding philosophy and not slowing down in its creative search; maintaining careful selection of its "mentors"; keeping the right balance between assisting and directing; abandoning old theatrical criticism but still evaluating its productions; delivering new talent and letting it go free into the world; never allowing the "training" element of its work to displace the emphasis on display, exhibition and performance for audiences made enthusiastic about "risk".

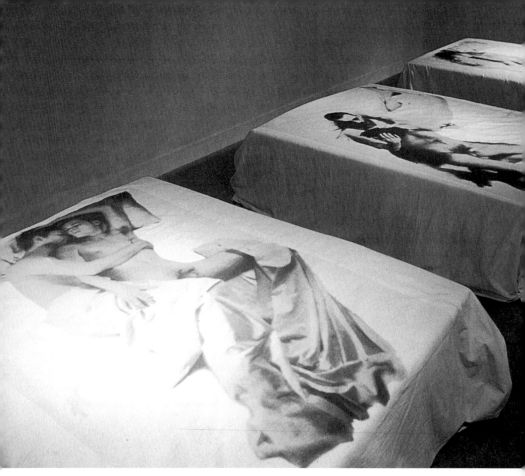

Above: Rory Donaldson - Generations of love (detail)

Right: Local newspaper headline

project    # Brenda and Other Stories...

artist    **Deborah Robinson**

Deborah Robinson (United Kingdom, 1962)
has been a senior exhibitions officer at
Walsall Museum and Art Gallery since 1991.

*Brenda and Other Stories* ... was a contemporary visual arts exhibition addressing issues around HIV. The exhibition was put on in 1996 by Walsall Museum and Art Gallery and later toured in the United Kingdom to Cornerhouse, Manchester and Nottingham's Castle Museum. The motivation to create the exhibition came initially from Deborah Robinson's personal experience which triggered an interest in the considerable artistic activity that had taken place primarily in the United States, where artists had played a key role in HIV campaigns - raising awareness and campaigning for resources. The numbers of those affected by HIV in Walsall are relatively low but it was still felt that such an exhibition would have relevance to local communities. Walsall has one of the highest rates of teenage pregnancy in Europe and previous monitoring of the gallery's audiences had shown that the most frequent attenders are the 18-25 age group, followed closely by children of school age - an audience that the *Brenda...* project was keen to reach. Research funding enabled Deborah to visit New York in 1994, where she met artists, activists, curators and others with an interest in HIV issues and to start planning what would become an exhibition within a project.

It was important that the project be seen within a broader context of groups, organizations and individuals working collaboratively to raise awareness of HIV and to provide a range of supports. So representatives of Walsall's health sector became involved and teachers were invited to attend consultation sessions which contributed to a formal education programme funded by Walsall Health Authority. The intention was to create a stimulating display

**33**

of high quality contemporary works of art that would simultaneously raise awareness of the facts and related issues around HIV, primarily, but also around sexual health and personal and social development. It was also hoped that the exhibition would provide a platform for discussion and debate and serve to extend the audiences for contemporary visual art.

The *Brenda...* tag to the exhibition came from a serenely beautiful yet powerfully disturbing work of that title, made by the artist Barton Lidice Beneš: two hundred, lined-up red ribbons (a symbol of HIV solidarity) made of heavy paper, coated with glue and breaded grey with the ashes of Brenda Woods, who had died of AIDS in New York City, in 1989. It was intended that the art exhibition should be open to different kinds of interpretation, avoid being didactic and try to keep a balance between giving children access to the aesthetics of art and to the issue of HIV/AIDS.

*Brenda and Other Stories...* brought together six artists from the United Kingdom, and four from the United States. The works spanned a variety of media, from painting through sculpture to installation. All of the selected artists made work with a positive outlook and a certain resilience and ironic irreverence in the face of the hated disease:

Barton Lidice Beneš, whose installation *Brenda* ... had been a major inspiration to the exhibition; Masami Teraoka, whose extraordinary paintings used the vernacular visual vocabulary of the Ukiyo-e woodblock prints and the language of Kabuki theatre to make contemporary portrayals of social issues; Stuart Netsky, whose work tended to focus around gay men's lives and experiences and themes of ageing, vanity and vulnerability; Ken Chu, artist and activist, working in multi-media and drawing on popular culture and gay "camp" aesthetics in both Eastern and Western traditions; James Barrett and Robin Forster, art²gº, whose show comprised 16 coloured photographs of magnified details taken from a male pornography magazine using a hole punch; Rory Donaldson, whose challenging yet tender, installation consisted of a red room containing four double-beds, each covered by a bed-sheet with a scanachromed image of a different gay couple, and complemented by a computer animation video; Derek Jarman, film-maker and painter, represented by a large, frenzied abstract piece produced by assistants under the artist's direction, when he was already in an AIDS weakened state; Lisa Z Morgan, represented by a fantastic machine, a distillery for liquid love, in the process of producing a magic potion to ameliorate all ills associated with the turmoil of love and including a number of different hand-blown glass flasks with seductive openings and sensual curves, containing bubbling pink liquid; Lee Birkett, who showed beautiful paintings of surreal landscapes inspired by aerial views combined with images of the microscopic workings of the human body, sometimes with "samples" from the texts of writer Jeanette Winterson.

A three-pronged approach was taken regarding the formal education programme. The exhibition was complemented by a resource pack aimed at teachers and carers and one of the artists worked in residence at a local school. Students were given an HIV awareness session in school before visiting the exhibition. They would then be visited at school by Women in Theatre who presented a production about a young couple, one of whom had contracted HIV. Additional resources included an information area providing a range of literature about the artists, other relevant exhibitions, some health information and a multi-media programme designed to introduce young people to issues around sexual health. There was also a publication and a free souvenir postcard containing basic information regarding useful contacts for further advice. All museum staff were trained in HIV awareness.

Deborah Robinson reported that just prior to the opening of the exhibition, a special press day was held to give reporters a detailed introduction to the exhibition. The visiting reporters appeared to be genuinely interested in the exhibition, so the museum was shocked by the hostile and vitriolic press and media reports that followed. Many of the press articles were incorrect and misleading, emphasizing the sensationalist and courting the controversial. As a consequence four of six participating schools withdrew from the project and the formal education programme was dismantled. However, once the exhibition opened, with a special viewing attended by the pop star Boy George, the visitors started to make their own responses known. The museum had never experienced such overwhelmingly positive responses to an exhibition. The comments books and response cards provided a platform for countering the initial press and media attacks.

**Lisa Z Morgan - The Ameliorative Love Machine**

The major contentious issue emerging from discussion of the *Brenda and Other Stories...* project has to do with the notion of commissioning artists to make art work on specific social issues. This is an issue which opens out to considerations of "the artist's motivation" with regard to a subject or piece of work, as well as to the potential for conflict between artistic and social motives in the approach to a piece of work. It emerges, of course that artists can identify a number of motives or, more accurately, starting points for their art works - a commission, inner drive, artistic ideas, ideals, social reaction, interest in giving or making art for young sensitivities and sensibilities. And there is much debate as to whether the good or great artist can make good or great art from any or all of these starts. Deborah Robinson argues that commissioning is always a negotiation between artist and commissioner - a partnership that can be mutually stimulating.

# Flickan, Mamman & Soporna

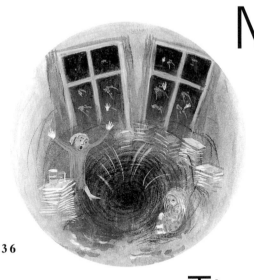

# The Girl, the Mother and the Trash

artist **Suzanne Osten**

Suzanne Osten (Sweden, 1944) has been artistic director of the theatre company Unga Klara in Stockholm since 1975, when she was asked to form a special division for children and young people within the Stockholm City Theatre. She has written a number of plays and directed several feature films. In 1995, she was installed as Professor of Directing at the Drama Institute in Stockholm.

**introduction**    Suzanne Osten, founder and director of the theatre company Unga Klara in Stockholm, is the author of the novel *The Girl, the Mother and the Trash* which has been adapted for Unga Klara by Erik Uddenberg. Suzanne had a childhood which shows parallels with the life of the main character of the novel, Ti. Her mother, the film critic Gerd Osten, became mentally ill when Suzanne was Ti's age. Although her mother continued working, she was quite distressed at home and could not accomplish the task of being a mother. In retrospect, Suzanne feels that the adults around her should have reacted to this situation much earlier than they did. She had already reached her teens when the facade finally broke down. Today, after more than forty years, she is still struck now and then by feelings of guilt and shame which she first felt as a child, over her mother's illness.

After achieving a success at the Stockholm City Theatre, Suzanne Osten was given the chance to form the theatre group Unga Klara. Suzanne selects her actors carefully and ac-knowledges that if her choices are wrong the production will suffer. She intends the ensemble of Unga Klara to be and work as a collective. The company sustains the child's perspective in its productions and takes on difficult subjects, since, for Suzanne, the power of theatre is to address things that are difficult to speak about in other ways. So, Unga Klara has courted controversy and experienced successes and setbacks. Suzanne admits to the fact that several of her plays have been flops, but she persists in taking on the difficult, the strange and the risky.

There are no velvet curtains at Unga Klara, because Suzanne is against velvet curtains. "To go to the theatre is still a matter of class", she says. "To reach an audience unused to going to the theatre is just as important a goal as it always was."

**presentation**    *The Girl, the Mother and the Trash* is the story about a girl, Ti, nearly eight years old, and her mother. Ti's mother says she is a prisoner, two invisible men are her jailers, the two demons Mr Polter and Mr Geist. In fact the mother is schizophrenic, but nobody knows about this - neither the mother herself, nor Ti. The only thing they know is that Mr Polter commands the mother to roam on the streets all day and collect trash. The trash is dumped in the flat. At night, Ti and her mother work till late sorting and labelling the trash. Since Ti and her mother live by themselves, daily life turns into a struggle for Ti: to go to school, to try to understand what is happening to her mother, to have some moments free from Mr Polter and Mr Geist, and, of course, to find some help.

The play has been performed by Unga Klara and the whole project involved cooperation with psychologists and support groups for children with mentally ill parents. These children, teenagers of around 14 years old, for once could be the experts, showing the actors what it looks like when a mother hallucinates, what kind of voice she may use, and so on. Another elucidating meeting was with two cleaners, working for a company that cleared and cleaned flats filled up with trash, dead pets and excrement. The actors playing the parts of the mother and her demons also visited a psychoanalyst specializing in psychosis.

Suzanne recalls one particularly significant event in the preparation of the production, which occurred when the ensemble was visiting a suburban school, improvising the first scenes of the play. After a while, they continued with discussion and improvisations during which the children could play the parts of the girl or the demons.

One girl wanted to play Ti meeting a very depressed mother. The mother of this girl was mentally ill. Looking at the improvisation the teacher, who knew the personal situation of the child, started to cry, but the girl continued playing. Then the class was asked what the mother should tell her daughter. They thought it should be something like this: "I have been possessed by two demons, and therefore I have not been so good to you. But now the demons are gone, and all is well". Suzanne confesses to having thought a lot about this girl since then - "I identified myself so much with her. Was it good for her that we came? I think it was. We became a kind of witness, without ever mentioning the word problem."

The Girl, the Mother and the Trash is performed for seven-year-olds upwards, preferably mixing different ages in the audience. It has proved to be very comprehensive and engaging even for young children. It is of course a very frightening story, albeit with a happy ending. Often the adults in the audience cry, while the children laugh. Children appear to be more matter of fact and less possessed by guilt than adults. Even so, Unga Klara take the time to "de-demonize" the actors for their audiences. They always have a little talk with the youth audience after the performance, speaking about the story and allowing them to take a close look at the stage design and the masks used in the play.

reflection    Clearly, with its disturbing and possibly horrifying content, The Girl, the Mother and the Trash, is a production that pushes at the limits of what are seen as suitable subjects to be treated in art productions for children and young people. Even at the research stage Suzanne Osten had some difficulty in finding children who would admit to experience of living with mentally ill parents. Psychosis proved a hidden illness. And just so, staging craziness for children also proved a problem. The solution lay in presenting two demons on stage as metaphors for paranoia and psychosis. The success of the play is important to Suzanne Osten, who hopes it will open up the claustrophobic world of mental illness, filled as it is with of secrecy and shame.

A part of the confusion in the debates over what is permissable for presenting to children turns on the question of "what is normal?" for them. Professionals, in and outside of the arts, have different interpretations of the question as well as different answers. For Suzanne Osten, a mother's and father's behaviour represents a child's concept of "normality". Which is why, she argues, children so easily grow accustomed to strange situations. In *The Girl, the Mother and the Trash,* the two demons order the mother to collect and sort out trash. The girl considers the collecting of trash as a normal thing. The mother has a strong relation with the demons. She loves them, she is even erotically attracted to them. Young children can relate to such demons. Most adults recall their own childhood demons, and, as Suzanne reminds us, psychosis is a mental illness that everyone can get. There are many children taking care of sick parents.

**M a u r a   D o o l e y**

# BETWEEN MUM
# AND THE WILD
# GARDEN

Recently I have been editing a collection of essays entitled *How Novelists Work*. The contributors were invited to write about how they started, their influences, their working methods and so on. Not surprisingly, many of them looked back at their childhood to find the source of their adult preoccupation, habit, career, magnificent obsession - call it what you will.

The poet and novelist Adam Thorpe describes how as a boy he would accompany his mother to work in the school holidays. She was the receptionist at an optician's in a small country town and while she worked out front, he sat writing stories in an old exercise book out back: "Now, to write a novel in the back room of an optician's, fronted by one's mother and ogling rows of spectacles, with the buttress of a wild garden at the back, strikes me as being rather memorably symbolic, but that's how it was. To write a novel is to don a different pair of spectacles, to test a different way of looking at things - and, of course, everything one writes is situated somewhere between Mum and the wild garden."

It seemed to me, that this engaging description of the mystery of writing, where it comes from within us, perhaps, unsurprisingly, also captures for me some essence of childhood itself. For where else can childhood fairly be said to reside, if not "between Mum and the wild garden"? And for those of us interested in creating and providing art for children and young people, isn't it our pleasure and our duty to inhabit that no-man's-land and to help map the journey across?

Many of these writers, and others I have spoken to, describe a childhood which has in it some element of suspended time, a proscribed solitariness: they lived in an out-of-the-way place, they were "only children", they had a period of illness as a child which kept them caged. I am not suggesting here that many writers are at best sad cases and at worst engaging in a kind of therapy - although the mere suggestion of this brings a knowing smile of recognition to many writers' lips. Certainly, writing can be a refuge. Rather, it has made me think about the workings of the imagination. It has made me consider its digestive system.

I grew up with television, radio, books, toys, a back garden and, at a time when it was still considered safe to play out in the street with other children, unsupervised. I was a very busy child but also ruminative. I liked time to mull things over and I had a rich imaginative life. In all the debate over "the new choices for young people", the single thing that worries me is the erosion of that dull, cud-chewing time. A time that for me, at least, I know provided the laying down of stuff, like geological strata, and that one day would result in my poetry.

Now, the zapping culture continuously feeds the recipient with an endless supply of fresh images, fresh entertainment. What I cannot come to grips with is whether this is an evolutionary change and therefore a marvel, or a behavioural change and therefore a worry. Do young people spend five times longer daily watching a screen than I ever did and still find time for reflection? Am I, in fact, the equivalent of those black and white films of yesterday's football stars, where the players run as if they've got treacle on their boots? Is it just, in short, that everything has speeded up? The logical extension of my anxiety would seem to be that we'll raise writerless generations, which is clearly nonsense, although I do think that there will continue to be a growing shift away from the printed word, as creative expression, and towards the visual image.

Yet, the spoken word and the printed word are of inestimable importance in my life. And like most things we feel passionate about, they only live fully and live on if we share them. As a poet I've visited schools, run workshops, judged writing competitions. I've spent years as an arts facilitator writing research papers, raising funds, sitting on committees, programming festivals, all intended to demystify the process of writing for children and adults alike. In this country, poetry in particular had been hijacked by the academic world and taken away from its old position, at the heart of the tribe. If it was taught at all in schools it was taught nervously and often badly.

Yet over the last 15 years it has crept back into peoples' lives again. I first noticed this after the fire at Kings Cross underground station in London which killed so many, including a fireman fighting the blaze. At his funeral another fireman read a poem he had written for him. Advertizing began to use poems, rap became a serious force, the film *Four Weddings and a Funeral* made W.H. Auden a cool commodity. When Princess Diana died last year poems were taped to the bouquets of flowers carpeting Kensington Gardens. There was expectation in the newspapers of a poem for the Princess from Ted Hughes, the poet Laureate, and a beautiful poem instead from Andrew Motion. How then, since the idea of the poem as a message in a bottle and the idea of the poet as spokesperson has somehow survived, can we make the quality match the sentiment?

It's about creative ownership. It's about saying to a child not only "you can do this" but you can be this". I have been involved in the development of the Writers-in-Schools scheme for some years. The idea is to arrange a series of visits by writers to schools up and down the country. The British school system is increasingly dominated by exams. Creativity is squeezed out. By bringing in a writer, a child or young person sometimes engages with the idea that a text has authorship for the first time. It can be a surprise simply to learn that not all writers are dead. The experience of meeting and working with an author won't make writers of all these young people but, as the poet Ian MacMillan told me: "Once, when I was a child, a brass band visited our school. It didn't make me take up the tuba but I've never forgotten that day and since then I've always known how a brass band worked."

One of the commonplace fears at the moment is that the glamorous, glittering world of computer games, Internet, film and video makes the idea of writing a poem or creating a play seem dull. I do not believe this. Telling stories is the way we make sense of this world. Every so often we reinvent our vehicle for doing this - the novel, the film, the Internet - but we never actually stop.

The "new technologies", which really can hardly be termed "new" anymore, have us at the heart of a revolution. Or is it in the slipstream, or is it at the eye of the storm? I'm so sick of being told about it that I've lost interest in its exact location, somewhere along that superhighway, but the experience is interesting. It is about possibility, variability and choice. It is about accepting change as a permanent state of being. The young person growing up with this has no problem with it, this is simply how things are. The older person must just get used to the wibbly-wobbly sense of a world that they had thought was flat but, no, look, it might just be round, or then again...

*Telling stories is the way we make sense of this world. Every so often we reinvent our vehicle for doing this - the novel, the film, the Internet*

There are perhaps two specific problems to do with the pace and scale of change. Firstly, the question of quality and secondly the matter of market manipulation. Youth are seen as a market to be both fed and exploited, both nurtured and milked. The speed at which the new technologies have been perfected has far outstripped the development of talented artists in this field. We are just beginning to understand that to produce work of any lasting quality in the new media, we will need to invest time and money, not only in the hardware and software but more essentially, in the people who use it.

Not much more than a century ago children were living through an invented genteel childhood if they were rich, or at work in factories, mills and on the streets if they were poor. Now childhood is both formally longer, in terms of education, and emotionally shorter, in terms of whatever we understand by the word "innocence". If in the past children in Europe were exploited as a cheap source of labour, down the mines and up the chimneys, now they are exploited as the providers of cheap labour in other countries. Our children can kick a football joyfully around the back garden, ignorant of the eight year old in an Indian factory who sits in a dark, cramped room packing the balls for a pittance. Our children can wear their favourite club's latest football strip, oblivious of the sweatshop in the Phillipines where other children have stitched it together.

Society is in a blue funk over what to think about children and childhood. Not a day passes without another news report of organized child abuse in a childrens' home or the revelation of yet another paedophile ring.

The latest fashion in confessional writings has led to a series of books concerned not only with the authors' own backgrounds but also with the bigger picture. Blake Morrison's *And When Did You Last See Your Father* which was about his own father and the father/son relationship was followed by *As If*, his examination not only of the Jamie Bulger murder (two eleven-year-old boys were convicted of the murder of a two-year-old boy) but also of the questions raised by the case.

Perhaps the Jamie Bulger case brought into focus, sharply, all kinds of notions and half-notions about what childhood is and what it is for. At the heart of the discussion, the analysis, the debate, the psychology, pop-psychology and cod-psychology, were real questions about the future of our society, but these went hand-in-hand with the sudden exposition of a media-manufactured terror about "video nasties". It seems to me that this is a very typically British response. Find something or someone to blame and outlaw it or them. Censorship.

The whole matter of what we deem suitable for children and young people is vexed. It is a problem in a number of different ways. For example, a responsible childrens' television programme might approach a particular subject, let's say teenage sex, differently from a soap, not made for a young audience but screened an hour later than the childrens' programme and watched by exactly the same audience. Meanwhile, the new film of "Lolita" opens with an "18" certificate, Adults only, but the book can be borrowed from the public library by any reasonably tall 12-year-old. The same subject matter on stage, would run into all kinds of difficulties if it presented itself as a young persons' show, yet that subject matter is the very currency of the playground.

Dr. Sonia Livingstone of the London School of Economics, giving a paper at the Second World Summit On Television for Children, in London, in March 1998, presented some figures illustrating European children's use of television and allied media. According to her statistics, in the United Kingdom 45% of 6-8 year olds, 68% of 12-14 year olds and 75% of 15-17 year olds have televisions in their bedrooms. This means that the majority of young people are watching television or video alone, without adult company. In fact, the television is commonly the babysitter. However, whilst more children here had personal televisions, fewer had their own PCs than in any other European country and whereas only 48% of children in the United Kingdom have any kind of access to a PC at home, in the Netherlands, for example, 85% have such access. The essential difference shown here is that television and computers are used by young people in this country for recreation rather than for education. The United Kingdom had the highest daily percentage overall of media use, with 9-17 year olds spending an average of 145 minutes per day on television, video, playstations or Net entertainment. A footnote to Dr. Livingstone's findings was that just as these figures increased, so time spent playing sports or reading decreased.

So why are all our young people supposedly lying in a daze amidst the cuddly bears and smelly socks watching *Sweet Valley High*, stuffing Big Macs, swigging Coke and forgetting how to read? And if that is the case, why is the British adult apparently not overly concerned? There are two obvious answers to this last question. Firstly, the United Kingdom has an honourable history of Public Service Broadcasting which may have resulted in the parents' touching but probably misplaced or out-of-date trust in the medium of television. Secondly, such is the level of anxiety about the safety of our children, at the moment in this country, that there must be a kind of collective sigh of relief, that at least they're safe up in their bedrooms.

Safe up in their bedrooms.... and receptive. Our children own something which is more valuable to manufacturers and merchandisers than almost any other commodity. At BBC Multimedia, they call this commodity "pester-power". That is, the ability to make adults part with large amounts of cash, by developing and exploiting arts and entertainments aimed at young people, through every conceivable commercial outlet. The new children's programming, which is developing through websites on the Internet, generates its revenue through advertizing more than through licencing. Increasingly, film, television and website productions are led not artistically or creatively but commercially. An executive for the American company World at Play, Jill Arnold, told me: "It's about education and culture but we can't deny we are a business. Our business is children." It's about making money. When my four-year-old daughter comes to the supermarket with me, she wants to know why I don't want to buy the Barbie baked beans, the Little Mermaid yoghurts, the Thomas the Tank Engine cakes, or the Lion King ice creams..... and we haven't even arrived at the world of play stations yet.

The effect of the market-place is more insidious and damaging than the slightly ludicrous presence of decal-festooned yoghurts might suggest. Boys are generally considered to have more spending potential than girls. Therefore, lately, several Hollywood film companies have decided only to develop family films which feature a male protagonist. One award-winning British novelist, Philip Pullman, was told that his feisty 13-year-old heroine might have to become a boy, if there was to be any hope of getting the film of his book made. This seems to me an unintelligent, ugly and depressing step backwards. Are girls not allowed to be capable, brave or powerful? Are boys not allowed to be vulnerable, suggestible or sensitive? Are boys and girls being given what television and film companies really believe they want to have? No, of course not. They are being allowed what makes the company the most money.

The power of marketing has had a great influence on children's reading habits too. The children's section of most bookshops in the United Kingdom contains rows of Roald Dahl, Enid Blyton, film and television tie-ins and series such as Point Horror or Goosebumps. These series, heavily advertised and promoted, are written by many different authors sharing one name to act as a kind of brand that children will recognize. They are a publishing success story and a creative nightmare. The books are uniform, predictable and linguistically unadventurous. They are the MacDonalds of the book world. Yet none of that would matter if the power of the publishing giant behind them did not squeeze out the variety and wealth available from other sources. One name, R.L. Stine, dominates 60% of all available shelf space in British bookshops. It is a great time for children's fiction in this country. In Anne Fine, Janni Howker, Philip Ridley, William Mayne, Philip Pullman, all established prize-winning writers, we have some of the most interesting, fresh, exciting voices in contemporary fiction. Yet with only 40% of the shelf space left for them and other less well-known writers, how many children may miss them altogether?

I began by quoting Adam Thorpe's description of writing, and I would say also, childhood, as inhabiting that glorious space "between Mum and the wild garden". It should be a voyage out. My worry is that we are encouraging a mono-culture so that wherever we are in this global village we eat the same things, dress in the same way, watch, play with, read and listen to the same things. Mum will always be there but where is the wild garden then?

*Maura Dooley (United Kingdom, 1958) is a poet who founded and directed the Literature Programme at the South Bank Centre in London from 1987 till 1993. She is also associate director of The Performing Arts Labs (new writing for young audiences) and writing cosultant to Jim Henderson Pictures. She has published several collections of poems. As an editor she contributed to books on poetry and literature. She was awarded a major Eric Gregory Award in 1989 and was shortlisted for the Forward Prize and the T.S. Eliot Prize.*

# Making the Future

artist   **John Retallack**

John Retallack (England,
1950) was artistic director
of the Oxford Stage
Company between 1989
and 1998. He is currently
setting up an experimental
theatre company for
children and young people
called Company of Angels.
He also serves as artistic
director to the Performing
Arts Lab.

In 1995 the Oxford Stage Company launched *Making the Future*, a phased theatrical initiative that aimed to bring the most visionary work for young people from continental Europe to the United Kingdom for the first time, in an attempt to improve the quality of theatre available to them. John Retallack, at the head of this imaginative intervention, had been long impressed with the achievements of theatre for young people in places like Holland, Belgium and the Scandinavian countries. In these countries well-subsidized theatre groups have been producing writers and performances of very high quality, touring to classrooms and sports halls in schools and fostering festivals of theatre for young people all over Europe.

In the United Kingdom, although many school children visit performances of the classics and see pantomimes at Christmas, they are not familiar with seeing exciting and innovative new writing and performance. John Retallack also registered that the above-mentioned type of funding available to these audacious theatre movements is not new. It has been in place since the 1940s, and, in some countries, for longer still. And John has argued that this funding commitment reflects a positive philosophy of child-hood in these countries that has been sustained through many changes of government. Accordingly, there are festivals of theatre for young people all over Europe - in Lyon, Berlin, Amsterdam, Copenhagen, and Stockholm; also, in the South, in Barcelona, and south of Rome there are more companies and festivals. In London, there is no festival, no "movement" as in Europe, where some of the best minds and imaginations are employed in writing, designing and acting exclusively for young people.

**49**

What struck John most was that much of this new and exciting continental European work was unapologetically imaginistic, or narratively complex, or boldly experimental. And all of it shared a common aspiration - to avoid naturalism and to find fresh means of expression. The resulting plays, he suggests, make children see differently and make us see children differently.

The Oxford Stage Company received a £60,000 award from the Vivien Duffield Foundation towards developing new audiences for the theatre which helped them to prepare and launch *Making the Future*. It took them two years. The award allowed them to afford the many rehearsal weeks that it took to prepare the plays that they performed and toured and to programme a number of associated events (discussions, debates, play-readings, residences, visits to schools). John Retallack intended that *Making the Future,* as it developed from 1995 through 1996 and 1997 might also do much to make theatre a forum for the discussion of contemporary issues.

The first programme of *Making the Future* was made up of three plays: *Hitler's Childhood* by Nicklas Radstrom (Sweden), *Mirad, A Boy from Bosnia* by Ad de Bont (the Netherlands) and *Grace* by Ignace Cornellisen (Belgium).

*Hitler's Childhood* explores the roots of fascist mentality with its twin foundations of ignorance and fear and illuminates the question: are we born evil or made so by others? It is a play which brings to life the imagined infancy and boyhood of Adolf

**Scenes from *Junk***

Hitler, showing the distortion of an innocent nature into a cruel and destructive one. It suggests the impressionability of the young child to persistently violent suggestion and denounces the stupidity of parents who direct their vexation at their own failure upon other races than their own.

**50**

The play *Mirad* presents the story of a 12-year-old boy's escape from Bosnia to a refugee home in Nunspeet (the Netherlands) and his subsequent return to the war zone to find his mother. Through the eyes of a young teenager we see how innocent people, including children, can be caught up in spirals of violence and revenge not of their making.

*Grace* is a charming, surprising and very funny comedy for children of 8 years old and above. It is an imaginative variation on the Cinderella theme, a blend of slapstick and magic, full of absurdist touches - the Prince has a heavy cold, the girl who loves him is nervous because she cannot count to 10 in French. Enchanting as "Cinderella", yet freshly minted.

*Making the Future II* consisted of 8 newly written plays, including two commisioned pieces, *Johnny Blue, Where Are You?* by Jane Buckler and a new adaptation of Melvin Burgess' new novel *Junk*. *Junk* is set in the 1980s and notable for its distinctive handling of drugs. The first part of the play "says yes to drugs", the second part tries to "get off drugs" and nobody dies. John Retallack believes that young teenagers today enjoy the great new "odyssey" of long and strange journeys, which is the kind of trip that *Junk* takes them on. Intended for teenagers, the play works just as well with 12-year-old children. The performances proved to be very successful and drew very large audiences. The BBC TV are screening the story in January 1999 and there are plans to stage an even more theatrically adventurous production of the play in the Netherlands. John Retallack's ambitions for *Making The Future* are being realized.

reflection    Oxford Stage Company's *Making The Future* has made what is almost a social mission out of a commitment to present artists of real imagination, who are determined to say something new and to make a difference, through children's theatre. Interestingly though, a project like this conjures up some of the most frightening bogeys for artists - exactly because of the explicit social agenda that is programmed in to its cultural intervention.

The major concerns turn on whether the funders of such interventions are funding artists to make direct social or pedagogical impact, or funding artists to make art that can make a difference in society. Most artists would shy away from the former and embrace the latter. The issue is particularly acute around art for children. For an artist like John Retallack his work must always be suf-ficiently free to permit him the grace of never having to present children with art that is cynical. Cynicism sets in when we give up our dreams, says Raul Atalaia. For the forthright Suzanne Osten, staging social problems is anathema. She believes that in our time, if one tends to pedagoguism, one is likely to lose the trust of children. She believes too that since schools often exist to put a moralistic and pedagogic image on everything that they transmit, then young people are unlikely to trust art offered them through schools. On that basis she could argue that schools should not aspire to plugging live art into the curriculum.

From her broader concerns of curating and commissioning art, museum curators like Deborah Robinson know that more and more special funds are being made available to artists willing to address social issues in their work. Increasingly then, "available funding" becomes a definer of art work, which can give rise to the conundrum of art made without primary artistic commitment. Arguably though, the artist of integrity can accept funding from anywhere and resist the programmatic pressures of funding bodies. Although, ideally, in art as in any other area of activity, funders should always be involved in partnership with the funded. Out of the experience of the Portuguese O Bando theatre-makers, Raul Atalaia has made a wonderful formulation of the funding dilemma for artists and art providers making work for children. He is of the opinion that the state has an interest in investing in artists as creators of "dreams". Of course, these dreams may be either inspirational or diversionary - and there's the rub.

# De Tasjesdief

## The Purse Snatcher

artist **Maria Peters**

Maria Peters (Curaçao, 1958)
graduated from the Dutch Film
Academy in 1983 with the acclaimed
short feature *Alle vogels vliegen*
(All Birds Fly). She is a partner in the
independent film production
company Shooting Star Film
Company. *The Purse Snatcher* is her
first feature film.

The film The *Purse Snatcher* by Maria Peters was the winner of the Glass Bear at the 45th International Film Festival of Berlin in 1995. It is based on an award-winning novel by the Dutch author Mieke van Hooft. Ten years after graduating from the Dutch Film Academy, Maria Peters read *The Purse Snatcher* and recognized it, as had others, as a great book for young people. Mieke van Hooft's novel had already been published in three languages and won, in 1990, the award of the Dutch Children's Jury and, in 1992, the Prix Européen de roman pour enfant.

The main character of the book, a schoolboy called Alex, is constantly forced by two older boys to do things against his will. The story shows to what extent someone who is pestered can lose their direction. Here, specifically, Alex is forced to steal purses from elderly women in the street but his broad predicament suggests something that can happen to any child. The poignancy is in that the cornered child does not dare talk about it with any-body. The book conveys this brilliantly. Alex enters a downward spiral from which he cannot escape. All his ways of finding help are blocked. He becomes completely isolated and the problem becomes too big for him. Mieke van Hooft's character enters the long nightmare of knowing that "As long as you keep silent, there is no solution". Maria Peters, who had worked for several years in drama features for TV and film, thought that the subject of the book was really suitable for a film and at the centre of her film she wanted to show children that they have to tell this kind of secret to someone - someone they can trust, be it a parent, a teacher at school, or, as chosen in her film, a grandmother.

The film was shot in 1994 - scripted and directed by Maria Peters, edited by Ot Louw, with music composed by Ad van Dijk. The Children's Jury report from the International Film Festival of Berlin in 1995 said: "... we selected this film because it is exciting and describes the reasons for the actions of the older boys. We also liked the film because it speaks to everyone and the performances are convincing. Alex was not understood by his parents but he could always go to his grandmother. This was a friendship which appealed to us. In spite of its serious subject there were funny scenes in the film; it is a film which makes you think how you would have acted had you found yourself in the same situation as Alex ..."

**53**

Maria Peters is convinced that there is a great need among children for films that tackle their own problems - taking them seriously, at the same level as those of adults. And she wants to do more work for children, since they make wonderful, honest and direct audiences - losing themselves completely in the story.

**presentation**    At the centre of Maria Peter's film *The Purse Snatcher,* Alex, a schoolboy (age 12), has some interesting and peculiar hobbies, like collecting and reconstructing skeletons of birds and small pets. He also plays the clarinet. He is an only child. His father is a travelling salesman in stockings and his mother is a beauty care specialist. Alex's parents are always busy with their work which pushes him closer to his grandmother, Roos (age 72). Roos lives in a secluded house on a dike near water. Alex visits her regularly.

One day he arrives at Roos' house to be confronted by a very rare phenomenon of a group of small frogs crossing the dike. Just as he enters Roos' garden to report the frogs, the front door bursts open and two boys rush out. They push past Alex and drive off on their mopeds, leaving many crushed frogs in their wake. Inside the house Alex finds everything in a mess and Roos tied up. She has been robbed by the boys. But Roos insists that Alex tells no one about the incident - not the police and not his parents. She is afraid that the incident may provide a reason for putting her into an old people's home - her idea of a nightmare.

The same evening, Alex has a phone-call from one of the bad boys, who was a class-mate, as it turns out. They agree to meet the next day. At this meeting Alex is threatened and hit by the other bad boy, the elder brother of his former class mate. And Alex reluctantly agrees not to tell anyone about the robbery and hopes that that will be the end of the business. Two days later, on his way to his music lesson, Alex meets the brothers by chance. They take his clarinet and suggest that he can earn it back by stealing the purse of an old lady. Alex runs off without his clarinet. The brothers call Alex again to tell him that he can buy his clarinet back. Alex finds that he has less pocket money than the sum they demand, but he tries to get them to accept it anyway. They don't and this time they do get him to steal his first purse in exchange for his clarinet, broken.

Alex cannot talk of any of this at home and Roos is still unwilling to broach anything to do with her original robbery incident. Alex becomes more and more isolated and the bad brothers continue to blackmail and bully him. When Roos slips from a ladder while cleaning and has to be taken to hospital, Alex feels certain that this is the work of the brothers again. He's had enough. He says no to any further dealings with the brothers. They grab him and threaten him

with a knife. They invade his bedroom and offer him a deal of regular weekly payments to them in exchange for no hassle. All he has to do is steal a few purses a week. Alex is reduced to stealing even from a blind woman. This has got to stop. But how will Alex succeed in getting out of this hell ... ?

In the original book by Mieke van Hooft, the grandmother takes control after Alex's confession. She makes him tell his parents and report the boys to the police. In her film Maria Peters draws out the process of the boys getting their due. There is an exciting chase through the school's dark corridors, where Alex knows the way but his attackers don't. Maria Peters says that she wanted Alex to take control after being bullied - to have some satisfaction. So that, although small and physically weak, he does have the courage in the end to act against injustice.

**reflection**    Maria Peters holds a personal opinion that a film (and by implication maybe therefore any work) for young people or children should have a happy ending. "One only has to take a look at the importance of fairy tales and stories from the Bible through the ages; good always conquers evil. This is what feeds the 'conscience'. Nowadays children are confronted with so much misery, one would not be surprised if they all become doom-mongers. Children's minds should remain flexible, they should not become depressed." There are other artists who deeply suspect this notion of message-work which explicitly takes on pedagogical responsibilities that can jeopardise the artistic merit of imaginative work. Some have even argued that Maria Peters' film would be more realistic, and therefore better in some sense, with an unhappy end. In another section of this text (see Raimo O Niemi) this debate is joined and broadened around responsibilities to children and responsibilities to one's art and engages with the idea that moralistic constraints on the artist may result in quality restrictions for the artist's work.

project **Liberdade**

**Liberty**

artist **Raul Atalaia**

Raul Atalaia (Portugal, 1952)
is one of the founders of
Teatro O Bando. His acting
and directing career has
been devoted to the work of
this company.

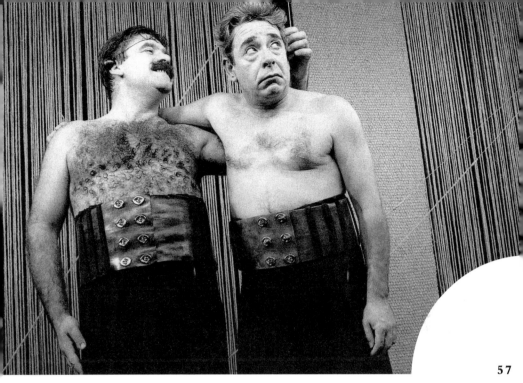

**Horacio Manuel and Raul Atalaia in *Liberdade***

**introduction**    The theatre group O Bando was created in 1974, in the "revolutionary" period that followed the collapse of Portugal's long standing dictatorial regime, which also signalled the end of Portuguese colonial empire in Africa. It was a period of rapid political and social change, with new things happening each day. Starting in the capital, Lisbon, the group consisted of a variety of artists who felt they wanted to do something for and with the people outside the cities. They were caught up in both the investigation and the building of a new sense of the whole of the culture of the people living in Portugal. Initially their project was dedicated, almost exclusively, to children and young people. The choice was born out of necessity as, at the time, theatre for children was of very low quality. But from the start O Bando never had audiences consisting of only children, which led them to decide to develop communitarian theatre, as a meeting place for all the generations.

The company has always had a strong interest in social behaviour - using its productions to critically address social issues and prevailing ideologies, often in some guise or other. This conscience-raising function within their theatrical work made them want to show, on an enlarged scale, the tangled human relationships and the conflicting forces that move in society. O Bando's productions feature the oppositions between work and unemployment, wealth and poverty, power and injustice - reflecting a reality that they, as artists, want to help change. Their work questions accepted truths, as presented in popular entertainment, by speaking out against isolation, speaking up for and reaching out to the weak in society - presenting human beings as social beings and emphasizing their inner contradictions over their social status.

While the group has achieved national recognition it also enjoys working internationally and regularly participates in festivals abroad. Each year they make one big open-air production and a number of smaller ones. For 1998, the big project is *Pilgrimage*, developed for EXPO 1998 in Lisbon. The show, a parade of spectacular, bizarre and amusing people-propelled mobiles, "scenery machines", is rich in symbolic meaning and involves 300 theatre-making performers from across the world - Europe, Africa and America.

**presentation** Today, O Bando consists of a 22-person collective. Aesthetically, its work is driven by a desire to popularize experimental and contemporary arts and stands on the two legs of animation and collective creation - revealing the anthropological roots of imagery to create the visually poetic. The creative process on a work begins with a proposal from a member put to the company. The spark may come from a piece of music; a social issue or a text, not always erudite and usually not written for theatre. Once the idea is embraced, the entire company - actors, directors, technicians and administrators - retreat together for a week, to a non-theatre space, to imagine an ambience for the creation. Weeks, maybe months, later the company returns to work on the creation, recalling ideas from the original retreat.

Like certain carnivalists, once a performance is over, the group loves to burn things so that the props cease to exist along with the performance. However, a few creations have survived their first performances and entered the company's repertoire. *Alfonso Henriques* is a compilation of medieval Portuguese texts, first performed in 1982, for audiences of six-year-olds to adults. The story seeks to humanize the heroic historical figures from the time of the first Portuguese king, featuring, for instance, episodes on growing up and relations with mum.

*Bichos,* by Miguel Torga, is an open air production, first performed in 1990, constructed around 14 stories of animals talking of their emotions and their feelings about humans. It is played by actors covered in clay, to audiences of all ages, with each performance taking its shape in part from the architectural environment of the place in which it is presented.

*Liberdade,* created in 1994, came forth out of a project performed in refugee camps in Croatia during the war in former Yugoslavia. It was part of *The Right Shoes,* a project of EU NET ART, which consisted of five plays of ten minutes each, made by five different directors from five European countries. The plays were about the rights of the child and all featured a pair of shoes. After the experience of these performances, the group felt a strong need to make a play about liberty. Not being able to find words to encompass "liberty", the text of this new creation is based on the poems of Sophia de Mello Breyner - amongst her lines:

> *The harvest has been reaped*
> *Now*
> *My solitude stands*

and:

> *She appeared and disappeared*
> *She asked the name of each thing*
> *Which name it was*

The themes of freedom, love and solitude are presented to children in the abstract but evocative language of poetry. The actors play in the guise of clowns, and the production employs the huge, wooden African marimba/xylophone.

**reflection**     As a theatre-maker with O Bando, Raul Atalaia sees his main responsibility as one of formulating questions about reality. He reasons that this is probably the best way to connect with children and young people - who are specialists in the art of asking questions. And, of course, he realizes that often the answer to one question is another question. So, in all of their work with children, O Bando's artists constantly question their attitude and behaviour. And they have come to ponder the possibility that where the child is seen too idealistically, the very idea of childhood itself becomes an abstraction. O Bando have discovered, as indeed all the participants in our discussion will have done, that the children in their audiences are their toughest critics. At the same time, particularly for artists pushing at the boundaries of experimental expression, children can provide the optimal artistic conditions for performance.

The O Bando questioning approach has even led, uncomfortably, to doubt about the pursuit of explicit political objectives in their work. Perhaps it is naive, and therefore childish in the worst sense, says Raul, to focus on dealing with social issues rather than dealing with the children themselves. Perhaps a truly liberated culture is one which allows its adults the freedom to occupy the spaces of childhood.

Pál Békés

# STRING
# OF
# TALES

*Against a background of permanent change*

All social changes, whether they are quick or slow, leave an
imprint on the minds of the people who are influenced by them.
And Central Europe is a field of constant socio-historical change.
To illustrate this, let me quote a popular Hungarian joke that has been
circulating in the area for a long time and appears in several versions
depending on who tells it:

A grandson asks his granddad about his turbulent life and he tells the boy
the tale of his journeys:

"I was born in the Austro-Hungarian Empire, moved to Czechoslovakia,
then went to the Soviet Union, back to Hungary, back again to the Soviet
Union and I retired in the Ukraine."

"Oh Grandpa, you have travelled a lot!"

"Me? I never left my birthplace, Munkács!"

The joke about the small town in the border area of Hungary/Slovakia/
the Ukraine which has a mixed Hungarian/Slovak/Ukrainian/Jewish/
Russian/Romanian population more or less describes the challenges an
individual has to face if they have been lucky enough to be born east of
Austria. In this century, in this part of the world, the most consistent
element of life has been inconsistency. This is the backdrop against which
we talk about children's and young people's reactions to the rapid social
and cultural changes in Central and Eastern Europe.

If we take a closer look at these changes, which the Western press usually labels as a period marked by the "pains of transition", we can see that a whole generation of children has been brought up amidst the tremors of a constant social-moral-psychological earthquake and a permanent revaluation of yesterday's truth: whatever was the unquestionable truth yesterday is a lie today. To give a "classic" modern example: children who were at secondary school between 1988 and 1992 saw a new history book published every year and those books reflected our modern history in different ways. I can hardly believe these young people were willing to believe a word grown-ups said by the time they took their final exams. This really is history in the making: they began school in an old, slightly crippled communist system and finished their studies in a new, nevertheless slightly crippled democracy.

The more or less closed, unchanged and politically controlled culture that generations of children were brought up with during the forty years of "existing socialism" was gone with the wind in no time. The "old-fashioned" egalitarian values were attacked, questioned and wiped out and in many cases the baby was thrown out with the bath water.

This process has been very similar - though with a lot of local colours of course - in most Central European countries which, with an ironical twist of history, doubled in number as a result of the swift dissolution of Yugoslavia, Czechoslovakia and the Soviet Union.

### The experience of yesterday

The forty years of children's culture was in many ways similar to the "grown-up culture": centrally censored and controlled on the one hand and heavily subsidized on the other. To give a grotesque example: the fifties, the "iron age" of communist rule, was the "golden age" of children's culture as many distinguished writers and other artists were pushed out of "serious literature" and were marginalized: they could work in fields that were regarded as unimportant by party bureaucrats, namely translation and literature for the young. The result was top-quality translated literature and children's literature. The process was similar in the visual arts - the best artists were restricted to the fields of animation, illustrations and the once very popular slides.

Later, when the "iron age" was over, these artists went back to "serious work", but many of them remained attracted to the children's world and helped keep up the standards. So the 1960s, 1970s and early 1980s saw a high level of less censored but still subsidized children's culture that was able to reach children all over the country. This is because there was only one television station reaching the whole of the population and there was only one big publishing house which had a strictly organized relationship with all the libraries and most of the schools. This period resembled a kind of late enlightened absolutism. Generations of children grew up with basically the same experience, with a very high level of art work or at least work done by artists.

At the same time a lot of elements of popular culture that Western people regard as their basic childhood experiences are missing from these generations. Even now I sometimes look blank when my friends from the United Kingdom or the Netherlands, France or the USA talk about their childhood experiences and I cannot react as a "normal man" as we didn't have cartoons (which for some obscure reason were considered bourgeois art) and hardly any Asterix, Batman, Snoopy and so on.

So these were the two faces of children's culture in Hungary, a country that - I do know - is very similar to all the other Central European countries in this respect.


### Culture today

As soon as the wind of social change that is usually labelled "the change of system" began to blow, the scene shifted radically. Censorship disappeared in no time - hand in hand with subsidy. Publishing of new works ceased

and Disney booklets flooded the bookshops and news-stands.
The Hungarian film industry collapsed (including the chance to make films for children), once-famous animation studios ceased to be independent and sold their capacities to huge American monopolies. Instead of the single, strictly controlled channel, children can now watch five new commercial channels stuffed with soaps. In fact, a media analyst recently counted that we can now watch 240 soaps per week on our screens.

So, that's it. Within a year or two all the characteristics, good or bad, of the previous decades have become a vague memory of the older generations and – without knowing it of course – children face the symptoms of an early crude capitalism that their parents never experienced. Westerners today don't remember this as their societies underwent this (unavoidable) phase a long time before.

It can be argued that if parents do not know how to cope with these changes, it does not matter – they belong to the past. However, this also means that parents will not be able to help their children make the choices from the possibilities that have multiplied in a very short time. The change of system was an explosion that old and young alike have faced unprepared.

### Television

At this point I must turn to television as this was the field in which *String of Tales* – the project I'm going to talk about in detail – took place.

Television has probably been the most controversial field of youth culture since its birth. As it started as a mass medium in the USA, reached Western Europe about a decade later, and Central and Eastern Europe a decade after that, we could assume that Europeans learnt a lot from the experiences of the Americans and that East Europeans learnt a lot from the experiences of those in the West. But – however logical this assumption is – no one learnt anything from anyone else. The problems, issues, doubts are more or less the same as they were at the advent of television. In what way could or should the wave of screen violence be limited? In what way could or should the young be prevented from the effects of the present tidal wave of aggression? There are no more correct answers than there were, let's say, 30 years ago. But no one doubts anymore that this is the most effective and most democratic medium that has been invented so far. Not necessarily democratic in the political sense of the word, but democratic in reaching both top and bottom of society at the same time; reaching everybody with the same ideas, offering the same information and the same – sometimes very questionable – values. Mass media – and let's emphasise MASS this time – is democratic by its very nature.

Anyway, the change of system resulted in an explosion in this field too. The "good old socialist way" (having one of everything that can be controlled easily) was over and several national and dozens of local stations began to compete. Statistically speaking, the time spent watching TV nearly doubled in a year, and the increase was the greatest for young people. Well, this is not surprising, but it is shocking. The collapse of national cultural production and the multiplied need of the new channels for cheap films ran in sync – the inevitable result was a flood of rubbish. And young people became glued to the screen without any guidance, or parental help or simply sober words as the grown ups were enchanted too and it takes time to differentiate between freedom and an overwhelming wave of rubbish.

### String of Tales

Amidst these sweeping changes, children's culture – as I have already mentioned – became a completely unimportant issue. If it was mentioned, it was as a minor slice of the market controlled more and more by the "multis" – just like many other fields of our new life.
One of the rare exceptions was *String of Tales,* a series on Hungarian

Television - the only surviving public one - from 1993 to 1997. Three
and a half years is quite a substantial time span for a programme like this.


### The interactive making of a tale

I happened to be both the inventor and writer of this series. It began as a
kind of "teaching course" on how to write tales. Originally, the idea was for
it to be purely fictional. But it changed in the process, and by the end its
social elements began to be as strong as the original fictional ones. And this is the point.

First we selected a group of children for conversations about tales. What are tales? How do
they work? What are the main characteristics? In what way does a tale differ from
other stories? These conversations and inter-
views were recorded and edited. When they
were broadcast we asked the children through
television to write us. To write what kind of
heroes they would like to see on screen and what
characters they would be happy with. The letters con-

*The collapse of national cultural production and the multiplied need of the new channels for cheap films ran in sync*

tained a lot of diverging ideas, so we selected the most probable
of them and offered some options - in fact a selection of possible heroes
- in our next programme. The children - the ones present in the studio
and those who watched us - decided by vote, so we got three
"democratically elected heroes" for our series: Bonifác the knight, Döme
his helper and Lilla their companion. The first one was a more or less
classic knight who tirelessly wants to right wrongs. The second was
similar, though not identical, to a popular hero of Hungarian folk tales:
the poor, clever wanderer, a bit lazy and always funny. The third, Lilla,
was an amazing mixture of a guardian angel who helps the two men and a
housewife. She had a straw hat that could make her invisible, thus saving
all of them from tough situations and, besides, she was an extremely good
cook. Even the names and the costumes of these characters were invented

or suggested by the children. We did everything we could to make them feel these three heroes belonged to them and represented them. But as soon as they were born out of the collective fantasy, they were set free and regarded as independent.

Even the first show, the first story that was about their "birth" was pretty successful. We received letters by the hundreds, all suggesting different moves for the heroes, different places or fields of adventures. Mostly individuals wrote their ideas, but sometimes entire groups of children, even school classes, sent letters. Step by step, our *String of Tales* became a nation-wide interactive game - when I use the word "interactive" I don't mean the computer-like interactivity of course.

*We did everything we could to make them feel these three heroes belonged to them and represented them*

Statistically speaking, most letters didn't contain really new ideas; some tips the children already knew from the tales they had learnt at school, read at home or seen on TV but many of them surprised us with their originality and individuality. And of course we tried to use these with some simplification of children's fantasy as financial pressure on youth programmes didn't permit us to use seven-headed dragons, dwarves and giants in every sequence.

The series was launched in autumn 1993 and as soon as it found its audience it continued more or less uninterrupted until spring 1997. The structure worked well and the children were willing co-authors of the stories that featured the selected and elected heroes. As it was broadcast at a really favourable time - late on Sunday mornings - at its peak it was watched by 4-6% of the entire population (10 million people) which could be interpreted (as media experts explained to us) as reaching 15-20% of the 6-12 year-old target population.

### Between fiction and reality

As has already been mentioned, *String of Tales* was intended to be a fictional programme, a series of short feature films based on the ideas of children. The characters invented and elected by our co-authors fitted in this approach too. Obviously the heroes weren't "intended" to face actual social issues, weren't "designed" to solve the everyday problems of children - only in a symbolical or metaphorical way if at all.

But the time when the series found its way to its audience was (and still is) an unusual period full of social tensions all over the country - and the wider area of Central and Eastern Europe - and consequently these problems began to sneak in to the letters of the children, and as soon as they appeared in their letters they had to be reflected on the screen in some way too.

More and more ideas and tales arrived that didn't place the heroes on the classical fields of tales, that didn't see them in Nowhere Lands ("over the Sea over the Glass Mountain where the short-tailed piglet lives" - which is how traditional Hungarian folk tales begin) but on the streets of Budapest or some other towns or villages and in the homes of the letter-writers. The heroes of our tale moved in the rooms of our co-authors. So we (the team) had to follow the *String of Tales* too.

One of the films we made was about poor people moving from one district of the city to another. The movers and their gang steal some of the furniture but our heroes get it back. In another film our heroes save the job of a father who is threatened by unemployment, a real worry for many families in the face of ongoing privatization. In yet another they repair the heating system of a huge housing area in a very tricky and funny way, thus saving the lives of the tenants. In fact the system is not broken but it is switched off because the debts of the community had piled up as a result of the unbearable prices of energy. In fact, about a third of the population of Budapest lives in apartment block areas of this type, a kind of council tenement, where they cannot switch off the central heating or minimize their consumption, and are therefore trapped in the ever-increasing price of energy which eats away at their income and savings and makes it impossible for them to leave - a huge social problem that seems to be unsolvable at the moment. And more and more films had to take place in slum areas.

So, step by step, the traditional enemies children meet in tales - evil dragons, black knights, jealous kings and other villains - turned into the more vague, even more threatening uncertainties of everyday life - the reflections of the overall uncertainty that surrounds us. And Bonifác, Döme and Lilla were "asked" and, in a way, "ordered" to fight these evils. Which they did uncompromisingly.

Still the three figures - we are talking about a television series - looked like classic fictional tale heroes in their colourful costumes although they had more modern duties. Through the mixture of traditional and new elements, fiction and social issues - *String of Tales* created a unique mix of reality and imagination.

By the time *String of Tales* reached the maximum "interactivity" this method permits, by the time it had become a kind of mirror of what 6-12 year-old children consider important in society, the series ended. The financial crisis of public television cut the *String*. This crisis had many causes - including competition, a challenge East and Central European public television had not previously had to face. When this crisis hit TV, the programmes for children were the first to suffer huge budget cuts.

The basic attitude hasn't changed yet. Children are less important. Culture for children is "not serious". Whenever a political statement is needed, culture for children is mentioned as a crucial field, and whenever cuts are necessary it is the first to be cut.

I am certain that after a while the real priorities of a healthy cultural life - and children must be among the top priorities - will take their rightful place. It might take time. I hope not too long, as we cannot afford to lose the minds of more generations. Either in Eastern Europe or anywhere else.

*Pál Békés (Hungary, 1956) graduated from Budapest University in 1980 as a teacher of Hungarian and English language and literature. He has worked as a novelist, a playwright and a translator. Presently, he is chief editor for literature and theatre at Hungarian National Television. As recipient of a Fullbright Fellowship he has done research at Columbia University and participated in the International Writing Programme at the University of Iowa in 1997.*

# The Berlin Children's Film Festival

**introduction**    During her time as director of the Children's Film Festival of the Berlin International Film Festival for the last 13 years, Renate Zylla has made a worldwide search for high-quality films for children (a core group of six to twelve-year-olds). The Children's Film Festival, which has existed for 21 years, is an annual event and presents new productions. There are two categories of films at the festival: feature films of at least 60 minutes and shorts (life drama and animation) of no more than 30 minutes.

Films invited to the festival are judged in competition by two juries. One, established since 1986, is comprised of 11 children of 10-14 years old, and the other is the international jury consisting of five adult experts. A large public (about 17,000 children over ten days) also has an opportunity to judge the entries. Their reactions and opinions are registered directly during the screenings, as well as in the discussions which follow each screening and by means of the hundreds of so-called "Mitmachzetteln" (children's written opinions) that are submitted to the festival organizers. In addition to sitting on their own jury which awards a Festival prize, active participation by children in the festival now includes publishing a Festival newspaper and the construction of a Children's Film Festival website.

The main priority in the selection of the films for the festival is that they should be of high quality - and a rough rule-of-thumb used by the festival organizers to judge quality is the success of a work in getting children to identify with the feeling or the characters in the work. But it is not uncommon for films to be chosen for their exceptional or unusual nature. So, not every film selected for the programme of the Children's Film Festival can be described as a classical children's film. Another important criterion for selection is that children should be challenged by the films. The festival values its flexibility and tries to avoid being strictly defined or classified.

rtist

# Renate Zylla

Renate Zylla (Germany, 1955) has been working with the Berlin Children's Film Festival since 1985, of which she became director in 1988. In 1990, Renate Zylla founded the Short Films Programme, an international selection of cartoons for children.

The Children's Film Festival was undervalued and marginalized at the point at which Renate Zylla became its director. Today, in its 22nd year, the festival's programme receives wide acclaim and its influence is growing still.

**p r e s e n t a t i o n**     The titles of the Children's Film Festival since the late 1990s have been: 1995 *The journey inside and outside;* 1996 *It's not easy to be a child;* 1997 *Allies for a day, friends till the end;* and in 1998 *Courage to act.* Renate Zylla believes that, increasingly, the selected productions of the 1980s and the 1990s have reflected the social situations which define and influence children's lives. Authenticity combined with convincing acting offer the children the opportunity to identify with the living conditions, feelings and suffering of others of their own age. Themes touched on in the films are, for example, separation of parents, unemployment, war and the fate of the refugee, loss of a parent through death, the search for a role model, poverty, violence and oppression, terminal illness. In each film, children are searching for happiness and allies, as well as for understanding and love.

**72**

Often the films are set back in time - in the Middle Ages, the 1920s, or the 1950s. But whatever the historical period, the big themes and values of friendship, love, honesty etc., continue to dominate the narratives. The deciding factor in communicating to children appears to be that stories be told from the perspective of the present even when looking back on past events. When a world is presented that can be experienced directly, children can be reached no matter what era is being portrayed. Children do realize that a time before their own has existed. So, for them, travelling through time is as important as a cultural journey to other countries. Both provide the child viewer with an insight into other ways of living.

Whether a film offers the possibility of identification is not dependent on how realistically it is staged. Feelings, moods and events can even be expressed in animated shorts, in such a way that the viewers are able to draw parallels with their own experiences. The film *Otto* by the Swedish directors Stig Bergqvist and Jonas Odell, for example, presents with wonderful sensitivity the easy incorporation of fantasy in the everyday life situation of a five-year-old. It is all about the fear of missing out on something, because he has to go to bed earlier than the others. In the fantasy world of the child, the most absurd ideas develop concerning everything that is happening and what the others are up to during the secretive evening time, when he should be sleeping. The directors clearly know this five-year-old and have reflected his feelings using a personal style (drawings, music, exaggerated colour designs). And the result is that the little ones in the audience recognize themselves in the situation of Otto.

Some directors work with their own childhood experiences, thereby coming to terms with their own un-coped-with feelings. The Danish director Aage Rais, for example, dealt with the painful loss of the father/grandfather in his film *Anton* (Denmark, 1995). Other directors work with the life experiences and fates of children who have touched them in some way, for example Renzo Martinelli in his film *Sarahsara* (Italy, 1993). Sometimes literary models are used as a reference.

For still others, it is the era in which they themselves were children that offers the inspiration. For example, the Swedish film Kannst du pfeifen, Johanna (Can You Whistle, Johanna,1994) based on a novel by Ulf Stark and set at the beginning of the 1950s portrays the time when director Rumle Hammerich was growing up, with a loving eye for detail. These directors want to tell stories which are important to them. They do not aim at a specific group. They create, above all, "their film". This means, paradoxically, that the decision concerning the target group that a film is intended for lies with the production and the evaluators (cinema distributors and those responsible for selection for television).

**73**

**reflection**      In spite of the undoubted difficulties and frustration in promoting and profiling her directors and "stars" in the mass media alongside the "real" stars who strut the stage of the big, Berlin International Film Festival, Renate Zylla remains enthusiastically committed to films for children. She is equally committed to encouraging and increasing the already considerable participation of children in the process of the festival.

The experience of the festival has shown that its selected films rarely receive further screenings. Distributors shy away from the dubbing expenses for foreign productions, subtitles demand too much attention from children and voice-overs tend to spoil a film. However there is no doubt that the films that are seen have a huge effect on children. And at the Berlin Children's Film Festival the children are centre stage and their opinions are collected, treated seriously and published. These commentaries are often attentive to detail and concerned with the "realness" of the works.

Of course in cinema, perhaps even more than in other art forms, it is important to consider whether the confrontation with specific harrowing themes may be too heavy for some children, particularly those who may have faced the situations portrayed in their own lives. But it should also be recognized that children can and do use escape into fictional worlds to distance themselves from their own lives.

project Kissan Kuolema

# The Killing of the Cat

artist **Raimo O Niemi**

Raimo O Niemi (Finland, 1948)
attended Moscow State University
and graduated from the Moscow Film
Institute (VGIK) in 1976. Between
1973 and 1997, he produced over 23
films, including short films, feature
films, documentaries and TV series.
His works also include four screen-
plays. He is currently completing a
feature film entitled *Poika ja ilves*
(The Boy and the Lynx).

**Scenes from *The Killing of the Cat***

introduction    In his early film career Raimo O Niemi followed the advice of his deeply revered master, Jean Renoir, who had said that in cinema "children and animals must be painted on the set". And he is still entertained by W.C. Fields' - "Anyone who hates children and animals can't be all bad". So that, up until 1985 Raimo had had only one previous experience of a child in the leading role of one of his films, and although everything had gone well, he definitely felt that children and young people should be left to others. Then, he was

asked to make a television series for young adolescents and, for the first time
in 30 years, began to read literature for children and young people in order to find
a theme. The result was two mini-series about a 12-year-old boy named Roi and a
German Shepherd. Since then, for the past 13 years, he has mostly directed and partly
scripted series for children and young people as well as films.

Working for means working with children and adolescents - people who are amateurs with
no training in acting or working on characterization. This makes casting a deadly serious
process. Because it is through its casting that a film will take wings, or turn out to be a
miserable flop despite all the efforts of its director. (In Finland, casting is usually the job of
the director. Raimo personally screen-tested almost 800 adolescents for *The Killing of the
Cat*, in order to select for just seven roles.) Directing young amateurs is also very different
from directing professional actors. It may take longer and call for more imaginative
techniques than those used with experienced film actors.

Although he has now benefited from years of experience, Raimo confesses that every
now and again he feels a need to work solely with grown-up professional actors. In spite
of the relatively meagre resources available - which means concretely less money, fewer
shooting days per project, less time to work on realizing one's vision, lower wages, and

despite the irritating taunt from insensitive commentators - "When are you going to make real movies?" - Raimo continues to make films for children and adolescents. He loves his job, in which he gets to work with enthusiastic, interested, untiring young people, who participate without whims and intrigue and with obvious enjoyment.

**presentation** Raimo O Niemi has the reputation of exploring challenging social issues in his films. But in the course of his career he has made an adventure series as well as love stories for TV. His first feature films *The Killing of the Cat* (1993) and *Tomas* (1994) did take on tough and difficult subjects, though - life in reformatories, sexual abuse, alcoholic parents, violence. *Tomas* deals, among other things, with teenage suicide. *The Killing of the Cat* deals with sexual abuse in a reformatory for young people - even if it has a happy ending. Raimo arrived at these themes mostly by chance, but he believes that there is no point in making things more beautiful than they are, particularly for young people who cannot be fooled. *The Killing of the Cat,* which was already a popular novel for young readers, came via his daughter's recommendation that he should make a film of it. With *Tomas* he was simply offered the directing job. For both films he was primarily excited by their good stories - their drama.

A son of the 1960s, Raimo has always been familiar with social activism and social issues, but in no way does he want to teach or preach in his films. On the other hand there is no point in glossing things over and painting a false picture of our world which he sees as becoming harder and harder. He would describe both *The Killing of the Cat* and *Tomas* as survival tales of a struggle towards light at the end of the tunnel. He is happy though if his films can provide some impetus for life or encourage confidence in facing the future.

**reflection**      Raimo O Niemi is saddened by the fact that few films are made in Finland for children and adolescents and that it is mainly films from the United States that are available to them, with only a small number of European films being presented, mainly on television. He points out that *The Killing of the Cat* was the first Finnish film for young people in 11 years. So he feels as though he is caught up in a kind of mission, drawing more children to watching Finnish films and so to participate in the vitality of their own culture.

Notions of "mission" and "social activism" infecting, so to speak, art practice are, of course, felt as threatening to the freedom of the artist as well as the quality of art work. Elsewhere, in this present text, Marlene Schneider argues that the choices made by artists working with children are necessarily informed by pedagogical considerations - even if it may not be popular or trendy to announce that one's approach is educational. Pierre Mertens, on the other hand, is prepared to state baldly that he suspects that if artists start out with a pedagogical message, they will end up with poor-quality art. Raimo O Niemi confesses that although he himself would never start, programmatically, to create art starting from a "message" or "mission", the great 1925 film and art work, *Battleship Potemkin* (director Sergei Eisenstein) would appear to contradict the Mertens' rule-of-thumb. Somewhere in this debate is the realization that what constitutes "pedagogics" changes over time and it is perhaps this that may determine whether an artist's work is pulled into the pedagogical field or not.

# Mohammed Benzakour

# IN SEARCH
# OF
# DON QUIXOTE

The birth of art is perhaps one of the most significant moments in human history, and aesthetics have proven to be an essential part of this. We need only think of the commotion caused by the repeated vandalization of Barnett Newman's paintings with a Stanley knife in the Amsterdam Stedelijk Museum. It reveals one of the best kept secrets of the art scene: the gaze of the spectator, even after thirty years of patient explanations in TV programmes, culture sections and museum education programmes, is in essence still guided by aesthetics ... and as courageous as was Don Quixote in his ideals.

Prior to the birth of art, only functional implements existed such as axes and spearheads, earthenware and jewellery. But these implements, dug up by archaeologists, are not capable of arousing our passion in the same way as the recently discovered frescoes under Trajanus' bath in Rome, or the awesome terracotta army located in the mausoleum of the first emperor of China, or the murals found in the Lascaux Caves.

Now, hundreds of years later, our planet has radically changed. The Industrial Revolution is an irreversible fact, the march of technology and computerization appears to be an indomitable process which brings bewilderment to millions. Previously, borders were practical and functional, now their only use is in a school atlas or a pocket diary and distance has changed into a fictitious, indeed, even virtual unit which takes shape as a number on a monitor. In short: I cannot avoid it, the world is a "global village".

Since the sixteenth century – more or less reluctantly – the Netherlands has been a country of immigration. Aided by globalization and internationalization, hunger, misery and genocide have brought about new waves of migration. Every day, refugees knock on the Netherlands' gates, after a torturous procedure, to continue their anguish in their three-metre square rooms in refugee centres, or on the eighth floor in an apartment building in Venlo.

Particular to the "New Dutch" is that they are not born in, but matriculate to the Netherlands; they were not saddled with this country, but chose it. Chose it, because the one – the "guest" worker – thought "the streets were paved with gold" and "Mercedes were as plentiful as chickens" here, and the other – the refugee – because he wanted to get away from the place where the rotting bodies, wailing mourners, rabid dogs and bloodied sand determined the street scene.

In the meantime, because of this rising stream of "ethnic minorities" the Netherlands has become a "multicultural society", a community of spicy chop suey and passionate rai music, of steaming couscous and minaret towers, of swinging head scarves and impetuous Afro-American rhythms, which should fill the native Dutch with pride and joy. But no, it has primarily led to much national scheming and many, many policies for minorities: policies aimed at a better future, with better education, a better job and a larger house for the pathetic, left-behind alien.

Despite its considerable failure rate, this patronizing policy is also applied, in a somewhat different fashion, in the realm of art and culture. Long ago the socialists believed that the task of art was to uplift the oppressed masses. This conviction is still alive and well; through the "socialization" of art and the increasing democratization of society the idea has been created that everyone has a right to their "own" art. As an extension of this the art institutes start taking into account the large diversity of cultural preferences; the cultural offering is expanded and made available to citizens in their own neighbourhoods.

Fine, you may think. However, the consequence of this is that Dutch policy towards minorities in the art and culture sector – the "multicultural art policy" – is aimed at a sort of institutionalized group identity, in which nostalgia is idealized and homesickness is subsidized; i.e. a policy aimed at the past. This policy seeks to strengthen Turkish identity, to confirm Moluccan unity, maintain the Moroccan heritage and reinforce Surinamese roots. All this must be aimed towards the special features of these groups, and if these features are not there, they are invented and fabricated. National programmes are designed which are aimed at the "development of individual forms of theatre from diverse ethnic groups" and a literary programme offers a "multicultural writing" course (What is your profession? I am a multicultural writer). Publishers attempt to grab hold of every person of colour who puts pen to paper and music, programmers endeavour ardently to include world music in their programmes. All this because ethnic art is in, or rather, because ethnic art is subsidized, i.e. brings in money.

Meanwhile, in the (literary) art sector a veritable subsidy circus has come into being for the ethnic artists and their "interest promoters"; the most important allocation criterion is the origin, whereby the degree of nostalgia, exoticism, rootlessness, estrangement, fragmentation and homesickness determine the amount of guilders. It used to be that an unhappy youth was a gold mine for a writer. This appears no longer to be the case. General misfortune is too indefinite, too vague; today whoever wishes to cause a furore as a writer must not only be unhappy, but more specifically a "victim". Success is set aside for those who write about the "misfortune" of being born a woman, or a homosexual, or a Jew, or more recently, a person of ethnic colour.

It is remarkable that since politics and cultural managers have decided that ethnic colour belongs in the public arena as a minority, and that it must retain its heritage, the ethnically coloured artists and their "interest promoters" have come to believe it as well: multicultural festivals in which specific ethnic features are collectively serenaded and tragic fates lamented shoot up like weeds. It is revealing that at such festivals it is always the councillor for minority policy who opens the event rather than the councillor for the arts.

Because of the fact that this practice is scarcely about the intrinsic or artistic value of the work of art, but rather about the eccentric values laid down from afar by policy-makers and politicians, and because of the fact that the inherent convincing and moving power of the art itself hardly matters, but rather the subject, the majority of these coloured artists and writers do not produce art but opportunistic art for mass sales. They search for the demand and then offer a prod-uct. Look at all the publishers with dollar signs in their eyes asking ethnic minorities in cafés if they would please like to write a book. Oscar Wilde said "All art is quite use-less", but it appears to be especially true for these "victims".

*It is, moreover, a question whether this "exotic kitsch" is the best introduction to art for children in a multicultural society*

It is, moreover, a question whether this "exotic kitsch" is the best introduction to art for children in a multicultural society. They will not only make up the audiences of tomorrow but will also be our future cultural and arts managers responsible for further shaping a harmonious multicultural society in which cultural apartheid and parochialism are outmoded conventions. We need a society in which work by migrant artists receives equal respect and awe, not a society in which children remember art by migrants as amusing entertainment by slightly weird and slightly pitiful people to whom you have to be just a little bit nice.

I think that art should not solely speak for ethnic minorities, women, homosexuals - or whatever specific group. Art from purely (quasi-) involvement is not art, but documentation serving as a source allowing historians to study a certain time period or culture - but no more than that.

This does not mean to say that involvement may not come from a tube of paint or inkwell or that involved art is by definition inferior art. After all, we need only remember how the Nigerian police are still searching for the Nobel Prize-winner, Wole Soyinka, whose literature was so dangerous to the recent dictators of his country. The literature of Havel and Konrad may well have paved the way for the dismantling of the Wall, to say nothing of the consequences of Multatuli's indictment against the abuses in the Dutch Indies. It is Huxley, Kafka and Orwell who still help us to this day to recognize and understand the reigning bureaucracy and "technocracy", an area to which Voskuil is currently contributing. Those who know the large lithograph How Whites Grow Big of Lucebert of 1992 know how white Western dominance works. Do you remember how the White House feared the razor-sharp songs of Bob Dylan in the Vietnam years, did you know that the legendary Moroccan band Nass El Ghiwane paid the price for its texts, critical of the regime, with the death of its leader Boudjema?

For all these reasons it is important that there is art which reflects politics and it is important that this art continues. What I am concerned with is that art is first and foremost concerned with stirring emotions, emotions through recognition if you wish. Naturally this has a strong personal connotation, rooted in the universal range of human emotions. I must admit that no matter how I shuffled around and played with various definitions and descriptions, I always came back to the definition of the writer Gerard Reve. He stated that art is: stylized human actions (or a product thereof) that stir emotions. The style used is also important, as according to him if there is no style, there is no art.

Social and policy categorizations such as validity, gender, age and ethnicity do not mean much in these views where Art and the promotion and perception thereof is concerned. Whether a painting has been made by a Greek from the 2nd century before Christ or by a Moroccan in 1998 who lives in the Bijlmer (a suburb of municipal housing in Amsterdam), should not matter; the individual who created the work of art should have nothing to do with the work itself. A good work of art is a work of art that is moving because it touches upon the truth and the truth can never be attributed to one individual, and certainly not to origin - it has no name tag or identity card attached to it. Ideally art should be just as anonymous as the truth. I believe that what is most important is what you feel when you see or hear a work of art, then what you think of it, and only then - when emotion is no longer part of the issue - the historical or cultural background from which the work of art originated. However, the concept of "multicultural art" brings the background to the fore, indeed, even worse, it has elevated it to be *the* evaluation criterion. In this way ethnic artists are seen more as a political product of the time and social context and as spokespersons for their ethnic groups, than as people with highly individual and artistic characters. In this type of climate is it right to ask whether Yo Yo Ma, as an Asian, can feel the white melancholia of Beethoven, Bach and their colleagues and, more importantly, illustrate this through his cello (as Mr Ma has converted to the Argentinean tango of Piazolla, this question becomes even more poignant).

No, politically correct statements and policy papers alone do not create a multicultural society, certainly not when segregation symptoms are taking hold like plague bacilli. A true multicultural society is one in which "multicultural" is an outdated term, something that speaks for itself, has become natural. Indeed, there is a reason why rai music is the most authentic and most successful illustration of multiculturality. It is spontaneity and harmony incarnate; beautiful Arabic songs and melodies played on Western instruments, such as rhythm boxes and synthesizers. It is hugely popular among the young, including non-Africans. No politician or manager came up with the idea of exporting rhythm boxes to North Africa.

The cultural institutions should not provide marginalized ethnic writers and artists with a podium, where they can wallow in their memories and their traditions, which appear so idyllic to the outside world. "Appear",

*Art and the criteria regarding what is and what is not art should no longer be naturally determined from one (Western) perspective*

because ironically enough the truth is different, far from idyllic: Moluccan stage actors immediately end their great desire to return after an initial visit to the Moluccas, Moroccan and Turkish writers turn out to be bitterly disappointed in their mythologized views of their home countries after having visited them for a month's holiday and Surinamese musicians do not want to return to the local dictator Bouterse. It is unfortunate that many of these young, ambitious writers fall outside of the policy; after all, they read Hermans and Vondel, they are fascinated by a fresh green Dutch village and have one silent dream: no longer to have to perform at multicultural festivals.

It should therefore be the task of institutions to create opportunities for self-development, to create an environment in which the character can be formed and in which issues such as cultural background and the formation of identity are redundant. In a multicultural society, moreover, art and the criteria regarding what is and what is not art should no longer be naturally determined from one (Western) perspective. First and foremost we need a meta-discussion on new art criteria rather than a debate on useless practice such as "multi-culti art". We need a society in which artists can profile themselves without the question immediately arising whether their art is "ethnic" or "native", but where the art is seen as just one form of expression among many. One would almost argue that art should ideally be seen and experienced with the innocence and purity of a child, because are children not the greatest and most passionate art lovers?

If this does not happen then I fear that the current multicultural art policy will continue primarily to create pseudo-artists, that circumstances will be created in which only Hamlets can thrive, characters who first and foremost are the incarnation of analysis, egotism and consequently of disbelief, scepticism. Characters who are continually aware not of what their duty is, but of the circumstances in which they work. We do not want Hamlets, we want characters who personalize their beliefs, their belief in the eternal, the undefinable, a silent surrender to a truth which exists outside of each individual and which moves them to serve and make sacrifices; we want those people who move people by fighting, who are enthusiastic servants of an idea and consequently surrounded by an aureole – we are in search of Don Quixotes. We want a Don Quixote because he is the embodiment of the cellist in Sarajevo who plays a sonata with all his heart in the middle of ruins while the city is bombed to rubble around him. We want a Don Quixote because he is the violin orchestra that plays cheerful tunes with heads raised while the Titanic sinks under the feet of the musicians ...

*Mohammed Benzakour (Morocco, 1972) studied Management and Sociology at the Erasmus University of Rotterdam. He is an elected member of the City Council of Zwijndrecht and serves on the Executive Council and the Literary Committee of the Rotterdamse Kunststichting (Rotterdam Art Council).*

# Hier Dort Irgendfort

## Journey into the Unknown

artist **Marlene Schneider**

Marlene Schneider (Austria, 1954) left her job as a school teacher in 1982 to become a drama teacher at the Landestheater in Linz. Since 1984, she has been working as a dramaturge at the Theater der Jugend in Vienna.

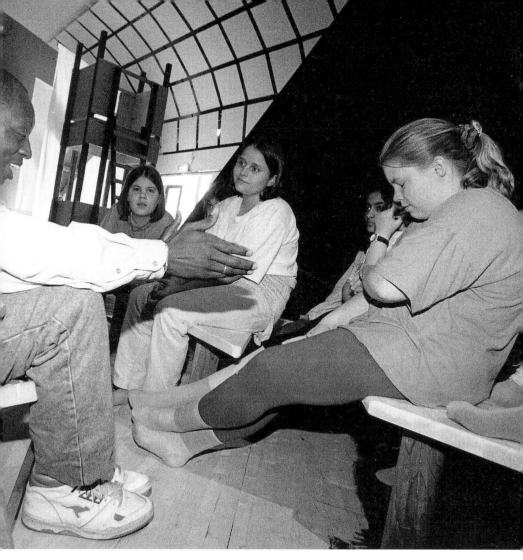

**The storytelling island**

**introduction**     Marlene Schneider, theatre and exhibition-maker, had already programmed five international theatre festivals for children for the Wiener Festwochen Festival when she was asked to develop an intercultural project for children on migration and integration. In the ZOOM Children's Museum in Vienna she found a place suited to implementing a novel interactive, multi-media project. The project, *Hier Dort Irgendfort* (literally Here There Anywhereaway) or *Journey into the Unknown,* was carried out in 1996.

Underlying the project were a number of contentious personal considerations on intercultural work and learning in the area of personality development:

The media room: projection windows place the children in different cultures

All those who work for children or convey art to children should be aware of the fact that art becomes political when consumed. Although this is irrelevant for the creative process of the artist, art always has pedagogical effects and is therefore political in its ultimate consequence.

Intercultural work should not focus on fighting prejudices but on recognizing prejudices in oneself despite the predictable discomfort this may cause. Only then can the next step be taken, to examine the use of prejudices in society and politics, to analyse their mechanisms and function and learn how to see through them. Most accepted intercultural and multicultural practice takes this second step first.

Intercultural work, with the best intentions, often falls prey to oversimplifications and distortions in the form of folklorization which shows us how beautifully different civilizations unlike our own are. The "exotic" is seductive, but what is truly exciting about the "exotic" is the ambivalence of emotions precipitated by the encounter with the unknown, the alien.

When it comes to teaching and imparting experiences in the field of personality development, which is one of the aims in making socially engaged art, Marlene Schneider believes in the importance of mobilizing one's own thinking, of repeated questioning, of the kick one gets out of searching for new answers. This seems to her a sensible way of disarming prejudices and

awakening a readiness to open up towards the unknown. She also stresses
the importance of challenging a great number of senses in the learning process - the stronger the impression, the more the brain memorizes.

The emotions can be harnessed to enhance learning. If sympathy and questioning can
be evoked at the same time, a decisive step in learning will have been achieved.

**presentation**      The aims of the *Journey into the Unknown* work were to impart to
the children an understanding of how difficult it is to leave one's own cultural environment
and to feel at home in a foreign one. Through the constructed intercultural, multi-media
and interactive encounter of the work, Marlene Schneider also sought to arouse the
children's curiosity about getting to know entirely different life concepts which they had
not even thought about so far. She had no intention of spreading a message in the work.
In the catalogue of the Wiener Festwochen she described the project as - "An encounter
with what is alien to us and what is alien in us". *Journey into the Unknown* is neither
theatre nor cinema, not an exhibition nor is it a performance, yet it is all of these together -
film, acting, photography, storytelling, light and sound are the elements of a guided tour
past three stations, lasting about 60 minutes.

**Shooting the video for the media room**

The first station consists of a "media room", about 35 m squared, the windows and
doors of which are neutral. Apart from the entrance, the room has a double door, four windows
and contains a TV set. When the doors and windows are opened they reveal screens for video
or slide projection. Loudspeakers emit sound, both at specific points and over the entire room.
A low pedestal seats approximately 30 persons. When the children come into the room, an
actress starts a performance in coordination with films seen in the open window and on the
TV. The actress performs the role of a woman in Turkey who has to leave her country. The
room is her house in Turkey. While the woman performs her daily activities in the room, the
children see the Turkish countryside on the video screens through the windows. In the same
action, the same room is transformed into the room of a house in Vienna, the city to which the
woman has moved and the video screens, through the windows show an urban environment.
The installation presents the children with the journey of a woman leaving home and coming
to an unknown country.

Leaving the media-performance room, the children are guided to a second station, the "storytelling island". Here they meet three people who have come from different countries and who
are now living in Austria. These people tell three personal stories of "there" and "here", each

gathering a group of children around them. The stories and story-tellers are presented in a manner that avoids stereotypes. One of them, for example, is a rich Black woman from Africa. The third and last station is the "slide labyrinth". Here the children can slide into various rooms which were not visible from their starting point and finally out into the open, allowing the children to themselves experience a journey into the unknown.

**reflection** Marlene Schneider is convinced of the importance of the emotions in social learning. She is intrigued by the ambivalence of the emotions which are precipitated by encounters with the unknown, the alien. It is these mixed feelings that she wished to evoke throughout the *Journey into the Unknown* work, making them so vivid that they would be fixed in the mind. She is convinced too that for developing awareness and enriching the development of personality, it is not enough to mobilize thinking in the form of discourse. The greater the number of senses that are challenged in a learning process, the stronger the impression left and the more the brain will memorize. She wanted to take the children inside an experience, to be part of its process. Hence the choice of an interactive multi-media format for this work.

**91**

She also specifically targeted children between the ages of 8 and 12, viewing these years as the time of changes and new orientations for children, where attitudes to danger and hostility to foreigners, for example, are fixed. She argues that children over 12 can be treated as adults, effectively, whereas for those under 12, the artist carries an unavoidable pedagogical responsibility. Younger children, for example, cannot be confronted with cynicism, as they will have no frame of reference for understanding it. She also observes that younger children do not select their own art. It is adults who take them to performances, exhibitions, films and so on.

In discussion, all of Marlene Schneider's personal approach to her work is contentious, from her views on art as political to her methods of engaging with what others call the multicultural and she calls the intercultural social terrain. Not all artists accept the constraint of her direct engagement with the pedagogical imperative for art work with young children which involves social issues or challenges. In another part of these discussions, Gerd Dierckx of RASA makes a hard distinction between the pedagogy of teachers and the methods of artists. But this does not necessarily imply any antagonistic contradiction with the position taken by Marlene Schneider. In her *Journey into the Unknown* work, she stands somewhere between the creative invention of the curator of art work and the creative imagination of the artist.

project

# Indianen van het Hoge Land

## People of the Bolivian Highlands

artists **Paula van Oostrum**

**Nilo Berrocal Vargas**

Nilo Berrocal Vargas (Peru, 1959) graduated from the
Universidad Nacional del Centro del Peru in 1983 and from
the Utrecht Art Academy in 1992. In Peru, he was active in
the University Theatre and made television programmes for
young people. As an actor and director he has worked on
various productions in both Peru and The Netherlands.
Paula van Oostrum (The Netherlands, 1960) is a cultural
anthropologist. She has been on the staff of the Children's
Museum at the Netherlands Royal Tropical Institute since
1994, where she is involved in research and programme
development.

**The diablessa dances with her knees up high, high, her costume glittering
like the precious silver and gold from the Bolivian Mountains**

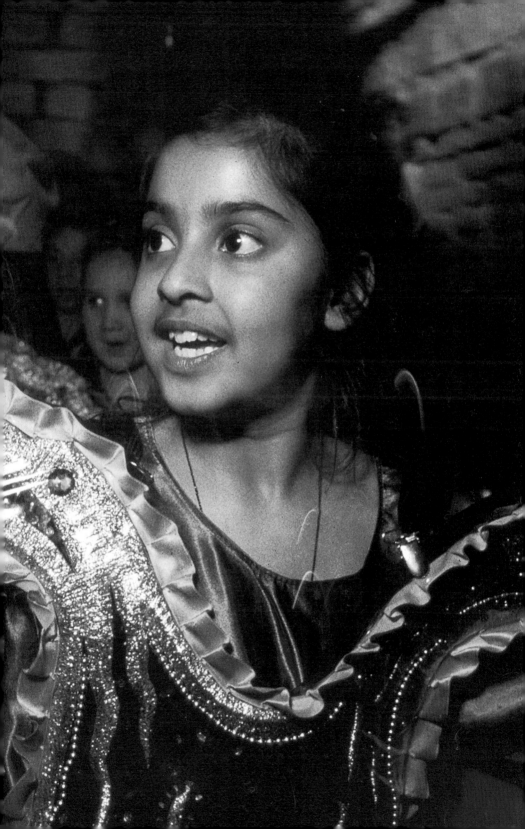

The Children's Museum at the Netherlands Royal Tropical Institute (KIT) in Amsterdam is an ethnographical museum for children of six to twelve years old and it operates within the objectives of the Royal Tropical Institute. It focuses on collecting, managing and studying objects belonging to the material culture of peoples in the tropics and sub-tropics. The age of the visitors has implications on the shape and content of the museum's exhibitions programme. Children who visit in school groups are provided with material related to an exhibition beforehand, which they can use to prepare for their visit. Individual visitors, who arrive without any preparation, are presented with a programme specially designed for them. The programmes are also adaptable for different age groups. Visits to exhibitions can vary in length, from one and a half to two and three-quarters hours. In all programmes the children themselves bring an exhibition to life. Introductions are organized so that they have very personal encounters with the objects and the tales within the exhibition. Staff members of the museum are always present as intermediaries between the collection, the exhibition and the visitors. Parents are only allowed into the museum in the company of a child who has just participated in the programme and consequently serves as the adult's guide.

**94**

The museum aims to arouse in its young audience a respect for other cultures, using play as a way to acquaint them with exotic cultures and complex issues. There is an attempt to present subjects as naturally as possible, without comparisons or linkages to the culture of the visiting children. In this way, it is anticipated that the children are left to make their own associations and conclusions.

The exhibition current in April 1998 was concerned with the culture, material and metaphysical, of the indigenous inhabitants of the Bolivian plateau in South America - about the ways they make a living, their way of life and their philosophy. A way of life dominated by the physical fact of living on a plateau, 4000 metres up in the Andes mountains, with a harsh climate. A philosophy which departs from the idea that contradictory forces in nature and social relations compete with each other and instead perceives them as complementary.

presentation    For the particular exhibition on the indigenous peoples of the Bolivian plateau, the Children's Museum organized a programme in three parts - 1. directed storytelling, with actors performing and functioning as guides to the exhibition installation; 2. hands-on activities with the children; 3. a festive meeting for children and their parents or adult carers.

The storytelling performances are used to introduce social and philosophical issues. And the

**The flutes are like inseparable brothers, together they weave a melody**

same stories form the framework for the hands-on activities. During these activity sessions, the emphasis of the exhibition experience is on personal encounters for the children. Using as much of the museum's collected materials as possible, the children are encouraged to touch and play with curated objects and to make their own objects inspired by what is displayed in the exhibition. To finish the programme, there is a festive meeting where the children and their adult companions enjoy presentations by the children of the experiences that they have gathered from the exhibition. Each group of visiting children is guided through the exhibition by three educational workers who play different roles - acting, dancing and making music. The intention of the museum is to present an exhibition that avoids the folkloristic stereotypes and to create an intense, emotional learning experience for the children.

## Introductory tale

*Imaynallata kachkanki pasnakuna huaramakuna noqa kani huaqaita tukuy tuky sonccoywan. In other words good morning boys and girls. Welcome to the Children's Museum. Inside is an exhibition about my country, Bolivia. In my country the mountains are higher than the clouds. The mountains are so high, you look like an ant if you are standing next to them. Even a big truck looks like a matchbox. In my country there are all kinds of fruits such as pineapple, mango, maize; even the potato of which chips are made, was born in my country. Long, long time ago the sun and the moon loved each other. But when the sun rose the moon went down, so they could not touch each other. And they cried with sorrow. Their tears were made of gold and silver and fell down on our earth. Then people came from the other side of the ocean and stole all our gold and silver. They forbade us to dance and to sing. Even our bamboo-flutes we were no longer permitted to play as well as our drums. Fortunately, the huge mountains remained. We keep on celebrating and our celebrations go on for weeks on end. In Bolivia nobody ever saw the sea. We are the only country in South America without a sea. But I wanted to see the sea, so I left. I walked for days and days and suddenly I saw an endless amount of water. I thought it was the sea, but it proved to be the Titicaca-lake, high up in the mountains. They even told me that it was the highest lake in the world. Some years later when I finally reached the sea, people called me "Indian". I did not know that I was an Indian. In my village nobody calls each other Indian. Everybody has a name; Carlos, Roberto, Armando, Nilo, Olympia, Maria. People wrote a lot about us, but nobody allowed us to speak. But now we are here to show you some things of our beloved country. We would like to have brought our feast, but the museum is too small for so many people. We even wanted to bring our mountains, but they are far too big. The enormous bird of the mountains, the condor, who wanted to come with us stayed there in the end, flying between the tops of the mountains. Hundreds of llamas wanted to come, but they stayed there and ran up and down the mountains. Nor did I bring the harsh wind, the starry heaven, the plains and the parrots. Nevertheless, we took some earth with us in blocks and we built walls of it. I took a lot of masks with me and costumes and instruments and many songs to celebrate. Welcome to this small piece of Bolivia. Watch, listen and enjoy the highland.*

**reflection**    For each exhibition presented by the Children's Museum within the context of the Royal Tropical Institute the curators are consciously confronted with the challenge of how to present another culture to young children without falling into the use of stereotypes. Fully recognizing that any culture is complex and cannot be represented in its authentic totality in a museum, the curators, the educationalists and the artists must make a selection of subjects and related materials and activities around which they create the narrative of the exhibition.

The intention is to turn upside down the normal museum presentation by bringing to life the objects through storytelling, dance and music. This is being attempted against a very challenging backdrop which consists of the same issues as are being faced by an artist like Marlene Schneider in her *Journey into the Unknown* work: breaking with the usual multicultural frame; engaging with personal prejudices and explorations of strangeness; exciting and agitating the senses in order to enhance the learning experience.

The Children's Museum, however, is working within the confines of museum ideology and priorities. Particularly palpable in the case of the Royal Tropical Institute is the weight of what might be called the colonial heritage which often hangs around the great museum collecting places of Europe. In spite of the best plans and hopes of the curators, these influences will have an impact on the presentation as well as the experience that visitors will have. In reality, in its encounter with "new world", South American culture, to which Bolivia belongs, European culture is exposed as rapacious, exploitative and genocidal. The story of the sixteenth century discovery and rapid mining of the mountain of silver at Potosí which the Cambridge historian J.H. Plumb famously described as "one of the turning points in Western history" (and which would have to make reference to the devastation of the native American peoples of the region, enslaved to dig out the valuable metal) finds but a limited and partial place in the Children's Museum installation.

The difficulty lies in introducing children in a contemporary European culture  to the knowledge that their cultural identities partly stand on such foundations. And what are the implications of not managing to include these difficult issues, for young children whom the museum acknowledges associate "far away" and therefore not closely connected to us, with "a long time ago" and therefore not still affecting our time and space?

"Tableau vivant" - *Charabang* (Pierre Mertens)

# RASA

**artists    Gerd Dierckx, Pierre Mertens**

Gerd Dierckx (Belgium, 1955) studied classical Indian dance. After having worked for
ten years in the educational department of the Museum voor Schone Kunsten
(Antwerp), she moved to Sint-Niklaas in 1989 to develop children's exhibitions for the
local museum. In 1993, she founded RASA, a production house for visual art projects
for children. Pierre Mertens (Belgium, 1953) is a visual artist who frequently makes
art works for RASA's exhibitions.

The word RASA originates from Sanskrit and means: "The mood or emotion evoked by experiencing a work of art". RASA is a production house from Sint-Niklaas, Flanders, that has been doing pioneering work in the field of art education for children, aged four to 12, for the past five years. Its activities include travelling exhibitions and the production of educational material about contemporary visual art - reaching 20,000 children a year. The combination of people and their know-how is what makes RASA unique. Passionate interest in the contemporary art scene, intensive contacts with selected artists, broad experience in the field of art education, group dynamics and the design and realization of projects, make each RASA concept into something special.

RASA aims to help children to associate with art because it allows them to see reality in new ways, to think in different ways - less straightforward and rational, more associative and emotional. Children are encouraged to participate in an active way, to go about discovering things for themselves and to identify themselves with the themes of art works - engaging with colours, architecture, poetry and dreams, working back and forth between what is seen and what is felt. And the experiences and emotions evoked by visual art can also be translated into movement, rhythm, sound and music.

**99**

Through its work RASA agitates, exercises and refreshes the senses, which act as synapses for the emotions. Pierre Mertens analyses daily reality and subsequently intervenes in it, through his work. Using all kinds of objects, employing painting, photography and video, he gives the ordinary a new skin. He dresses and at the same time accentuates reality by isolating it. A Pierre Mertens exhibition is always an adventure involving risk. He creates new work, on the spot, for each exhibition, searching for connections with the visitor as well as with the site of the art work - the social context and the art scene. He is particularly interested in the social relevance of art exhibited outside the known art circuit, "there where common people live".

**presentation** The RASA works presented to the expert meeting took a variety of forms intended to pose a number of key questions about the possibilities offered by art for children: the social importance of art for children; the ability of art to break with the images of the everyday life of a child; the usefulness of art in creating a forum in which children can talk about social problems; the position of the artist whilst working with children.

### Children's Portraits - Willebroek (Pierre Mertens)
Willebroek is an industrial municipality between Antwerp and Brussels, inhabited mainly by industrial workers. The local, active youth workshop invited Pierre Mertens to set up an

exhibition starting with the children and in confrontation with their work from the workshop. Mertens made a selection from available material and created new work together with the children. He let the children register themselves and their surroundings on video. He made a composition of school photographs of their parents of 15 to 20 years before and confronted the children's images with different materials and contexts. The variety of developments of this project led to an intriguing exhibition.

### Charabang - Borgerhout (various artists)

*Charabang* was conceived as a counterpart to the official arts programme of "Antwerpen 93". Artists visited different "problem districts" in the city and were invited to work in confrontation and/or collaboration with the inhabitants. Photography was to be the central medium. Pierre Mertens was invited to conceive viewing objects. The inhabitants, youngsters included, were invited to participate in different ways - submitting album photographs of their family and community feasts and parties to be reproduced for display; making self-portraits for exhibition; making "portraits" of the switched on television screens in their households; participating in "tableaux vivants" where they played themselves. The artists were responsible for presenting the results in the streets and squares of the locality. It was important that the inhabitants should be able to respond to and comment on these results. The project asked questions and revealed problems about the particular sociology and anthropology of the local community which seldom gain attention in the polarized discussion about immigrants.

### Eight leaves for an exhibition - Artificial Flowers (various artists)

RASA developed an educational programme for the exhibition *Artificial Flowers* at the Provincial Centre for Contemporary Art in Hasselt, Belgium. In a special room, the children discover a huge flower painted on the floor, around which they can sit. They become involved in a philosophical discussion on art as the theme of the exhibition. They also get an explanation about eight linen bags that are hanging on the wall. In these bags they find the material needed for their tour around the exhibition.

For *Artificial Flowers*, artists from all over the world were selected. Although the theme of the exhibition was beauty, one of the artists, Eric Lamouroux, focused on the banality of everyday life. He presented blowups of amateur pictures which confronted the spectator with a raw reality show. He is fascinated by the non-explicit meaning of the photographic image. RASA created a photo game, intended to let the children discover the differences between the images of daily life in these amateur photos and the deceptive appearances in photographs meant for publication.

Pierre Mertens insists that there is no art without a dialogue. This is particularly true for "plastic art" as distinct from "performance art", since, for him, "plastic art" has to be effectively re-integrated with the real world, real life, real livers. The project *Charabang* brought contemporary art to children and young people in what was once an industrial boom town. And he reported that the project certainly engaged with and provoked a response from within the community. The most explicit reaction was the destruction of the outdoor exhibition of photo-works, made by and with members of the community.

**"Portrait"** -
***Charabang***
**(Pierre Mertens)**

Concern as to why this piece of art evoked such a violent reaction ranged across consideration of cultural, racial, artistic and social contradictions. For Pierre Mertens though, the search for communication embraces confrontation with his audience, the art scene and even with the people involved in a project. So although interested in discussion of factors determining particular responses, none of that deflects from the necessity of risk and adventure in the search for communication through art.

Gerd Dierckx re-stated RASA's commitment to working with artists like Pierre Mertens who create projects that invite children to think and talk about art and everything that they experience while seeing an exhibition; thus bringing an existential dimension to the objective of making art accessible to children. So, showing social reality does not of itself lead to more awareness about the reality depicted. Children should first be intrigued, as they are when confronted by beauty, fantasy, poetry and the stuff that dreams are made of.

Gerd Dierckx threw up two imponderables for discussion. First she raised the implication of the fact that a child will never buy an art work, so that, in this sense, there is no art market for children as there is for adult consumers of art. This is of course something that could change with shifts in definitions of participation for children (an issue raised in Pál Békés' contribution to the discussions), as well as through innovations in marketing strategies. Secondly, she underlined the fact that the methods used by the artist and by the art teacher will never be the same. Artists have other goals, a different drive.

European Cultural Foundation
Jan van Goyenkade 5
1075 HN Amsterdam, The Netherlands
tel: +31.20.6760222
fax: +31.20.6752231
http://www.eurocult.org
email: eurocult@eurocult.org

Foundation Arts and young People in Europe (EU NET ART)
Keizersgracht 462
1016 GE Amsterdam, The Netherlands
tel: +31.20.6249683
    fax: +31.20.6239975

        KIT Press
        P.O. Box 95001
        1090 HA Amsterdam, The Netherlands
        tel: +31.20.5688272
        fax: +31.20.5688286
        http://www.kit.nl
        email: kitpress@kit.nl

        Children's Museum, Royal Tropical Institute
        Mauritskade 63
        1092 AD Amsterdam, The Netherlands
tel: +31.20.5688.233
fax: +31.20.5688.331
http://www.kit.nl

Oxford Stage Company
15 - 19 George Street
Oxford OX1 2AU, United Kingdom
tel: +44.1865.723238
fax: +44.1865.790625
http://www.Oxfordstage.co.uk

RASA
Dr. Verdurmenstraat 16
9100 Sint-Niklaas, Belgium
tel/fax: +32.3.7768688

A d

**Shooting Star Film (Maria Peeters)**
Prinsengracht 546
1017 KK Amsterdam, The Netherlands
tel: +31.20.6247272
fax: +31.20.6268533
email: shooting@xs4all.nl

**Teatro O Bando**
Rua Santo António à Estrela, 60
1300 Lisbon, Portugal
tel: +351.1.3953289/90
fax: +351.1.3970626

**Unga Klara**
Box 16412
103 37 Stockholm, Sweden
tel: +46.8.50620370
fax: +46.8.50620371
email: andersfrennberg@stadsteatern.stockholm.se

**Victoria**
Fratersplein 7
9000 Gent, Belgium
tel: +32.9.2253732
fax: +32.9.2250076
email: victoriatheatre@compuserve.com

**Walsall Museum and Art Gallery**
Lichfield Street
Walsall WS1 1TR, United Kingdom
tel: +44.1922.653116
fax: +44.1922.632824

**ZOOM Children's Museum**
Museumsquartier, Museumsplatz 1
A-1070 Vienna, Austria
tel: +43.1.5226748
fax: +43.1.5235886
http://www.tØ.or.at/~viezoom
email: viezoom@tØ.or.at

| Coordination | Erica Kubic (EU NET ART), Veronie Willemars (European Cultural Foundation) |
|---|---|
| Final editing | Colin Prescod, London |
| Copy editing | Louise Bolotin (European Cultural Foundation) |
| Production | Ciska Kuijper (European Cultural Foundation) |
| Graphic design | Ris van Overeem, NAP, Amsterdam |
| Graphic design cover | Nel Punt, Amsterdam |
| Translation | Hogg Translations, Brussels (texts by P. Békés, M. Benzakour and T. Ziehe) |
| Printing | Veenman drukkers, Ede |

Photographs and illustrations

*p. 28:* Phile Deprez

*p. 29, 30:* Kurt Van der Elst

*p. 32, 33, 35:* Gary Kirkham

*p. 36:* Anna Höglund

*p. 38, 39:* Lars Peter Roos

*p. 48:* Hugo Glendinning

*p. 50:* Sheila Burnett

*p. 52,55:* Shooting Star Filmcompany

*p. 56, 57:* Mariano Piçarra

*p. 71:* Berlin Children's Film Festival

*p. 71* (cat girl): Ronald Siemoneit

*p. 74, 75, 76:* Claes Olsson, Oy Kinoscreen Ltd.

*p. 87:* Didi Sattmann

*p. 88, 89:* Bernard Mayr

*p. 90:* Georg Herrnstadt

*cover, p. 93, 95, 97:* Liesbet Ruben

*p. 98, 101:* Pierre Mertens

**104**

This book is published in a series by the Royal Tropical Institute on museums and cultural policies. Previously published:

- *Art, Anthropology and the Modes of Re-presentation: Museums and Contemporary Non-Western Art* (1993), edited by Harrie Leyten and Bibi Damen
- *Cultural Diversity in the Arts: Art, Art Policies and the Facelift of Europe* (1993), edited by Ria Lavrijsen
- *Illicit Traffic in Cultural Property: Museums Against Pillage* (1995), edited by Harrie Leyten
- *Intercultural Arts Education and Municipal Policy: New Connections in European Cities* (1997), edited by Ria Lavrijsen
- *Global Encounters in the World of Arts: Collisions of Tradition and Modernity* (1998), edited by Ria Lavrijsen

This book is also part of a series of publications by the European Cultural Foundation within the framework of the programme *Art for Social Change*. Previously published:

- *Truth or Dare. Producing Theatre with Young People from Diverse Cultural Backgrounds: Practices, Examples and Pictures*, Royal Tropical Institute (1998)

A forthcoming publication in this series will focus on art projects with children and young people who have been confronted by violence. This publication will be edited by Chrissie Tiller and is scheduled to appear in 1999.